A COMMONSENSE REVOLUTION

BEN MURRAY BRUCE

Introduction

My name is Ben Murray-Bruce, and I have always been guided by Common Sense. My Common Sense story, the Silverbird story, began with my father Mulligan Murray Bruce, who started Domino Stores fifty five years ago with only one store in Yaba and by the 70s had grown it to become Nigeria's largest indigenous supermarket.

I worked in that very first shop as an assistant and it was there my dad passed on to me my first Common Sense principle of life which is that hard work multiplied by anything equals success in anything you put your hand to do.

And speaking of my dad, I was such a precocious son. While I worked at Dominos, he would always catch me dancing. Sometimes I would be dancing the funky monkey, other times I would be dancing the camel walk.

Finally, he warned me to stop dancing and focus on serous things or he would break my leg. But I just could not stop dancing. And not just that, I felt that dancing was serious business.

Any way, out of respect for my dad... No, let me be honest, out of a strong desire not to lose my legs, I suspended dancing until I went to the US in the 70s for my undergraduate degree at the University of South Carolina after which I settled in Los Angeles.

It was there that I met Don Cornelius, the creator and host of Soul Train who taught me another pillar in my Common Sense philosophy.

Don was fond of saying that "when you come up with a good idea, you don't have to do a whole lot, the idea does it for you".

I came up with the idea of giving Nigeria world class entertainment at a price my people could afford.

CommonSense was what inspired me, in 1980, to create the Silverbird Entertainment Group with a 20 Naira share capital secured from my father and siblings, amidst the austerity of the Shehu Shagari administration.

Despite the doomsday forecasts of failure offered by everyone I pitched the idea of Silverbird to, Common Sense told me that my idea would succeed, and Silverbird Entertainment Group did succeed, because in the midst of the economic uncertainties of that era, entertainment was exactly what the Nigerian people needed to escape their bitter realities and find joy again in life.

This Common Sense is not unique to me. It is a trait apparent in all Nigerians. Our national Common Sense is known it by different names - some call it hustling, survival instinct, or aggressiveness, but in truth it is an innate wisdom that when properly channelled, allows Nigerians to survive and thrive in the midst of any adversity.

When people ask me about my education, I tell them I have a Bachelors degree in Business and a PhD. in Commonsense. This may be true for most Nigerians.

Commonsense is what led to the creation of Nollywood at about the same time I started Silverbird and is responsible for making it the third largest film industry in the world. It is also the reason that Nigerians dominate the list of the most successful and influential Black people in the world. It is the reason why I know that though we are facing difficult times at the present moment with our economy and with issues such as terrorism and militancy, Nigeria will not just survive but she will also thrive.

Nigeria will not become rich if we produce and sell more oil. It may already be a cliche, but nations do not grow rich by what they have under the ground. Rather, the wealth of nations today comes from what her citizens have between their ears. In our case, we have an astute and creative common sense.

One of the men God used to make me into what I am today was the late Vice Admiral Joseph Akinwale Wey.

As a child, Vice Admiral Wey took a liking to me and taught me that I could achieve anything I wanted to achieve in Nigeria if I would always see every Nigerian as my brother and sister.

Even though the administration he served as de facto number two created states, he told me that Nigerian states were mere children of necessity and that we are all brothers and sisters born from the womb of one Nigeria.

And he was right.

Today, if you ask Nigerians where General Gowon is from, very few people really know because both he and Vice Admiral Wey were so Nigerian that you could easily believe that they were from any where in Nigeria.

And that is how I see Nigeria. I am from Nigeria. I am from your village and your town and that is why I want a constitutional amendment to replace state of origin with state of residence. Achieving this would be the crowning glory of my Common Sense Odyssey.

And I believe that with a Common Sense Revolution, Nigeria can effectively mobilize all her resources and pull herself up to be the leading nation in Africa in all ramifications - economically, diplomatically, and militarily as we creatively use our talents to bring into existence industries and solutions that did not exist before.

I have been to almost all African nations and what I have consistently been told is that the continent is waiting for Nigeria to take the lead and that will not happen if all Nigerians do not consider it their responsibility and duty to contribute towards making this happen.

These are some of my contributions in that regard and I hope they will inspire you, the reader, to make yours contributions towards the achievable greatness of Nigeria.

-Ben Murray-Bruce.

FOREWORD

The fact that Nigeria has recently surpassed South Africa as the largest economy on the continent of Africa is testament to the ingenuity and energy of its people.

Now in this thundering call to those very citizens Ben Murray-Bruce lays out a compelling narrative and details the path necessary for Nigeria to rise beyond its oil based economy and the corruption of its leaders and launch a common sense revolution to achieve greatness and the nation's full potential. Declaring forcefully that no matter how much oil is in the ground, Nigeria's true wealth resides in what is between the ears of every one of its citizens, Ben Murray-Bruce reveals the common sense steps government, industry and individuals need to take for Nigeria to take its rightful role as the leader in creativity, wealth and innovation across Africa.

The central truth in this book and revealed by Ben to all who will read his words is that it is the common sense inside every Nigerian that will provide the energy and dynamism that launches Nigeria into the future.

Ben's mission to unleash every citizen's potential reminds me of Barack Obama's emergence onto the world political scene with the simple words "Yes We Can". Like Obama in America, Ben's message aims to engage every Nigerian to join together and use their common sense to change government, create better institutions, new businesses and a brighter future. One has to hope that Ben's words and deeds can inspire the same energy among the young people of Nigeria that Barack Obama was able to inspire among the young people of the United States. Ben's message? Its your future, seize it.

Perhaps there is no better example of the common sense revolution than Ben's own personal story. With literally nothing but a share capital of 20,000 Naira from his father and siblings and the dream of starting an entertainment company, he pitched his idea everywhere. And just about everywhere he was told no. I t could not be done. Doors were shut. Most thought his dream impossible, impractical, and shunned investing in his enterprise. They could not see what Ben could see Today Ben's dream is reality, his Silverbird Entertainment Group is a reality and Nollywood is known throughout the world. He may live modestly but he is independently wealthy beyond even his dreams. And where too many today have public lives that look successful while their private lives are a shambles, Ben's family life mirrors his public success. All built on his reliance and belief in his own common sense. His dream now for Nigeria's future relies on his belief in the common sense of all Nigeria's citizens.

The beauty of Ben's book is that he effectively communicates his ideas in simple and understandable language. He somehow has taken the ambitious goal of making Nigeria the leader economically, diplomatically and militarilyamong all African nations and outlined the path to achieve those goals in a book that is assessable to every citizen and in language that can be understood by all.

There comes a time, a tipping point, in every nation when old problems pile up and hold a country and its people back from its destiny of greatness. Such times demand a vision that seeks a new way. Governments and parties over time become corrupt, not just in the sense of bribery or cronyism, but also corroded like an old car battery that has been rendered useless by the corrosion caking up around its terminals - government can get stuck in the old ways. That kind of corrosion can be just as damaging to a nation's future as the sorruption we usually associate with governments. Both on occasion demand that the people must be engaged in the clean up and the rebirth of a nation's progress to a brighter and bolder future.

In his sweeping analysis Ben Murray-Bruce provides the vision of a Common Sense Revolution for all Nigerians to build that brighter and bolder future. From tackling the problems of tribalism, Nigeria's archaic Visa system and failed fuel subsidies that hold the nation back to his forward looking solutions of building Nigeria's brain infrastructure, creating a new politics beyond the old parties empowering the nation's youth and harnessing new technology and entertainment to chart Nigeria's path to greatness Ben Murray-Bruce has taken the brave step of challenging the past and shining a light on the future.

His message could not be clearer - Nigeria's Common Sense Revolution begins today and it begins with you. And like Barack Obama his message to all Nigerians is *"Yes We Can"*.

—*Joe Trippi*

Liberté, égalité, fraternité
Land, peace, bread
Labour isn't working

The ability for three words to communicate so much has been born out through history and unleashed some of the most powerful revolutions the world has seen.

A "Common Sense Revolution" by Senator Ben Murray-Bruce is also three words with the potential to fundamentally change the future of a country, but with more in common with the type of peaceful revolution created by Thatcher than Robespierre or Lenin.

There have been many times when the words 'a new type of politics' have been uttered only to be a fleeting moment of optimism before everything reverts to type.

However there is something remarkably fresh and new about how Ben Murray-Bruce has caught the public's imagination in Africa's most populous nation. He is not the 'common man', to do what he has done is indeed most uncommon, but he has managed to touch a nerve and communicate to the people of Nigeria in a way that has reached out to all irrespective of State or religion.

Communication is not just about speeches, oratory prowess or, even in today's world, how well you tweet. It is a two-way street where it as important to listen as well as to speak.

The very title of this book is testimony to that as it emerged from a trending hashtag, #commonsenserevolution that was created by the people of Nigeria in response to Ben Murray-Bruce's ongoing narrative on events based on his simple theme of: "I just want to make common sense".

Ben Murray-Bruce heard the people and acted. And we can see that in how he addresses each issue where he combines leadership with responsiveness, to create quite a unique and powerful blend of communication.

Time and time again he hits the bullseye across the nation, whether it is challenging Ministers to reduce government waste by, for example, not flying First Class or donating his Senatorial Clothing Allowance to impoverished women. These individual actions are not unrelated topical or tactical initiatives but are informed and driven by his very clear belief in the need for the very fabric of Nigerian society to change.

At his speech at Silverbird Group's 35th Anniversary he made the case clearly and powerfully that the biggest division in Nigeria is not between North and South or between Muslim and Christian, but between Rich and Poor.

With the peaceful transition of power in 2015 the people of Nigeria have seen that their vote can count, but unless they see the benefit that change will count for nothing. Ben Murray's Bruce's current contribution is to hold to account a Government that promised change so that the people's hopes and aspirations are not dashed once more on the rocks of 'politics as usual'.

As has already been pointed out, Nigeria recently surpassed South Africa as the continent's largest economy. What is less widely known is that by 2019 it will be more than twice its size and will be one of the world's top 20 economies. Ben Murray-Bruce believes it is Common Sense that the common man should finally share in this prosperity and if not we will see a different type of Revolution that will make what happened in France over 200 years ago look like an amuse bouche.

I have been to Nigeria 46 times and have been hugely impressed by the intelligence, ingenuity and exuberance of every Nigerian I meet, but who for so long has been manacled by a corrupt elite and ineffective government. And in Ben Murray-Bruce the people have been impressed by a man who they believe can help free them to realise their potential.

Ben Murray-Bruce's vision is to create a Nigeria where every citizen will be judged not from the State they come from but where they are going. Ben Murray Bruce's Common Sense Revolution is to show how Nigeria can become a country where, to paraphrase Cicero on Rome, everyone will be able to claim "Civis Nigerianus sum" and expect – and deserve - to be treated fairly and equally.

—*Michael Moszynski*

Table of Contents

CHAPTER 1:
A NIGERIA FREE OF TRIBALISM

I was very angry on Friday, 23rd of October, 2015. One of my Twitter followers had tweeted a photo of an advertisement for a room to let. What was disturbing about this to let sign was that the landlord had listed a long list of tribes that he would not rent out his premises to. I would not offend the sensibilities of my readers by listing the tribes blacklisted by the landlord, but I must say I was mad as hell after reading his post. How could Nigeria have gotten to this level?

But then again, when I reflected on the matter, it occurred to me that we are all to blame for tribalism in Nigeria. First of all, we do not have any mechanism for fostering national cohesion which would be the only lasting panacea for sounding the death knell to tribalism. You might ask yourself what about the National Youth Service Corps (NYSC)? If you do not know that that noble idea introduced by General Yakubu Gowon's administration has been badly bastardised, then you need a massive dose of reality to cure your reality distortion.

In today's Nigeria only the most naive undergraduate does not know that it is possible, for a fee (read bribe) to 'sort' your posting to a state of your choice. There have been verifiable accounts of individuals who have served in their own states of origin. There have even been provable cases of individuals who went abroad for their Master's degree while they were meant to be serving Nigeria.

And so without any first hand interaction amongst Nigerian youths to enable them know about the people and tribes that make up this blessed land, many of our youth rely on biases fed to them by their friends and family. As such, with the only mechanism we have to build a detribalised Nigeria distorted, the fault lines of division by ethnicity and religion continue to widen. And what is more, we seem to have an aversion to history in our curriculum.

The other day I was talking to a young Nigerian business owner of 42 years of age who did not know that Nigeria had fought a civil war. This young man went to good schools and graduated from a well reviewed second generation Nigerian university. If he does not know, I can only imagine how much more ignorant of our national history those younger and less educated than him would be. In response to my followers' tweet, I released a series of tweets with the hashtag #killtribalism and I was pleasantly surprised that in less than an hour that hashtag became the number one trending topic in Nigeria according to the official Twitter trends. That the issue trended so dramatically made me realise that our youth (who largely determine what trends or does not trend) are hungry for the right information.

Basically, this is what I tweeted. Many young Nigerians do not know that the first elected Mayor of Enugu was a Fulani man named Malam Umaru Altine who was elected to that exalted office in 1956. Malam Altine was loved by the people of Enugu and at that time they would probably have stoned anybody that refused to let out his property to Altine on the basis of his tribe or religion. Malam Altine's case was not even unique. In 1957, an Igbo man, Felix Okonkwo, was appointed a member of the Northern House of Chiefs. So integrated was Okonkwo into Kano's society that he was better known in some areas as Okonkwo Kano.

This detribalised politics was not only limited to the then Eastern and Northern regions. The Western region also practised it. In 1950, an Igbo man, Mboni Ojike, was elected Deputy Mayor of Lagos. And I must commend the people of Lagos State for sustaining this welcoming and all embracing attitude to all Nigerians in 2015 by electing Chief Oghene Egoh, Mrs. Rita Orji and Mr. Tony Nwoolu as their representatives to the House of Representatives in the 2015 general elections even though they originate from other parts of Nigeria.

Tribalism, regionalism and religious intolerance were strange to post independence and early independent Nigeria and you and I have to bring back that Nigeria. That is the only way that all Nigerians can be at home in any part of Nigeria without being regarded as settlers in their own country. That is the only way we can kill tribalism, regionalism and religious intolerance before it kills Nigeria. The constitution recognises anyone born in Nigeria by Nigerian parents as a citizen. We must go the next step and accept any Nigerian resident in any part of Nigeria as a full fledged citizen with all the rights that indigenes of that area have.

We must amend our constitution to criminalise discrimination of any Nigerian citizen in any part of Nigeria because he is not an indigene.

Indigenes and residents must pay the same amount for school fees and social services all over Nigeria. Every Nigerian must feel at home in any part of Nigeria. Ironically, while we are so focused on divisions by tribes, ethnicity and religion, the rest of the world is breaking down these barriers.

At the 2015 Conservative Party conference, British Prime Minister David Cameron showed just how far his government is willing to go to make Britain a home for all. Cameron urged British employers of labour to do more to eliminate the discrimination of people whose ethnic origins are not British.

Said Cameron: "Opportunity doesn't mean much to a British Muslim if he walks down the street and is abused for his faith. Opportunity doesn't mean much to a black person constantly stopped and searched by the police because of the colour of their skin. I'm a dad of two daughters – opportunity won't mean anything to them if they grow up in a country where they get paid less because of their gender." Continuing, Cameron condemned a true life situation where "one young black girl had to change her name to Elizabeth before she got any calls to interviews".

Now juxtapose this to our situation in Nigeria where a state governor sacked civil servants for no other reason than because they were natives of another state. What is bad is not just that this governor sacked these innocent civil servants. No. The worst cut is that he was applauded for that inglorious act. In one of my first back page columns for THISDAY, 'Death to Xenophobia and Tribalism", I wrote about the rage in several African nations over the xenophobic attacks on fellow Africans by South Africans.

Is it not hypocritical that while we condemned such behaviour, we are treating each other worse back in our individual countries? Or is it only tolerable when we do it to ourselves? Only last week, I was looking at the data from the world renowned US venture capitalist firm, Kleiner, Perkins, Caufield and Byers, and their data revealed that 40 per cent of Fortune 500 companies were founded by first or second generation immigrants. But that is not the story. The story is that many of these immigrants were denied a level playing field in their countries of origin which forced them to seek more equitable environments in the West.

The number one obstacle which militated against these mega successful people from reaching their potential in their home countries was a lack of social justice. Nigeria has an acute shortage of medical doctors and nurses and other health personnel, but there are more Nigerian doctors practising in the United States than there are in Nigeria. The story told by one of our doctors in the Diaspora paints a graphic picture of why many of our best brains leave Nigeria. This young man had grown to become an expert in his field of medicine and one day he was scheduled to perform surgery on a VIP. During the post Op, he found out that the man was a former Nigerian leader. After a successful surgery, the former First Lady thanked him profusely and wondered why he was not practising in Nigeria.

It took all that the young man had in him not to lose it and go on a tirade of how, through policies like quota system and federal character, he had been denied opportunities at home which were then handed over to him on a platter of gold by the nation the First Lady was asking him to leave. I have written about the tribalistic tendencies inherent in some Nigerians, however, if truth be told, some of these tendencies are fostered by the government through policies like quota system and Federal Character principles.

How can youths be loyal to a country where their cut off mark in the University Matriculation Examinations (UME) and common entrance depends on their state of origins rather than on their intelligence? Invariably what the government is telling these youths is that where you come from is more important than what you know. In short, that your state and your tribe is your identify rather than your country. I am in Calabar for the Most Beautiful Girl in Nigeria 2015 pageant as this piece is being written and watching these lovely beauties from all over Nigeria interact with each other without regard to ethnic and religion, I am moved to say that Nigeria does not have hundreds of tribes. Nigeria has only two tribes. Good people or bad people. No more, no less. Let us kill tribalism together!

Finally, I congratulate Miss Anyadike Unoaku, also known as Miss Anambra, who has emerged as the Most Beautiful Girl in Nigeria 2015 (MBGN). Congratulations and may your reign usher in peace and prosperity to Nigeria.

My name is Ben Murray Bruce and I just want to make common sense.
Published: 2nd November, 2015.

Chapter 2
Of Ethiopian Airlines, Cut Off Marks and Patriotism

In my last back page article for THISDAY, entitled 'If You Build it They Will Come', I had evangelised for Nigeria to develop some of the potential foreign exchange earners we are currently not tapping and for which we have a very good comparative advantage. I had singled out the aviation industry and tourism. I wrote in that piece about how certain nations had shifted their economy away from resources to services, writing that "by opening up her borders to the world, the UAE's economy has more than doubled and though she is an oil rich nation, over 30 per cent of her Gross Domestic Product (GDP) comes from her aviation industry. Between 10-12 per cent comes from the tourists industry. This is a total of over $180 billion per annum!

Since I wrote that article, there has been a positive development that vindicates what I had written. Only yesterday (August 24th, 2015), Ethiopian Airlines announced a revenue of $2.27 billion. To put this in perspective, this is more than the total budget of Nigeria's richest state of Lagos. This amount also dwarfs the total projected income from oil that Ghana expects to earn in fiscal year 2015 ($1.5 billion).

The announcement by Ethiopian Airlines corroborates the statement I made in that last article to the effect that "to put things into even more perspective, oil is not a renewable resource. It has a shelf life. It will finish one day or lose value sooner than that. But tourism is a renewable resource. It will always exists. As an economic mainstay, it is safer than oil!" Indeed, tourism and its allied industries like aviation, are indeed safer than oil as an economic mainstay.

The question however is what is Nigeria doing right at this pivotal moment in our history to generate such headlines as that generated by Ethiopian Airlines for Ethiopia? Everywhere Ethiopian Airlines flies to (including to

Enugu and Abuja), she is positively projecting the image of Ethiopia. As I have previously written before, no one buys your product until and unless they buy your culture and there is no better way to spread your culture than with a national carrier. I dare say that Ethiopian Airlines does more for Ethiopia's diplomatic ambitions than any or perhaps even all of her embassies combined. The question is, why can't Nigeria build and sustain her national carrier? The answer, to my mind, is the 'Nigerian Factor'!

Yes, the Nigerian factor. Do some research on Ethiopian Airlines and you will find that it is professionally managed with its board chosen without regard to ethnicity and religion. It is run in a businesslike fashion. Ownership is separated from management and the result has been growth that has resulted in Ethiopian Airline becoming the most successful airline in Africa, making 300 per cent more profit than South African Airways and more money than all the other African airlines combined! But Ethiopian Airlines did not write this playbook for airline efficiency. No! They learnt it from Dubai.

Emirates do not even employ the best the United Arab Emirates has to offer. No. They employ the best the world has to offer. Fly on any Emirate Airlines flight and you will be impressed by the quality of their air host and hostesses. They always boast that on each flight, they have nationals from multiple nations.

Even the Chief Executive Officer of Emirates Airlines, Sir Timothy Clark, is not from the UAE. He is British! That is how far the UAE has placed professionalism over ethnicity and the result is that professionals have built their airline and their aviation industry from a tiny airline that started off in 1985 with two airlines leased from Pakistan International Airlines to become perhaps the most successful aviation industry in the world with over 500 planes and operating over 3,300 flights a week from the Dubai International Airport. Even though it is foreign professionals that built their aviation industry, who is the money made from the industry coming to? It comes back to the people of the UAE.

What killed Nigeria Airways and almost every other national corporation that should have been a national asset? We brought in ethnicity and religion into these organisations and staffed them on the basis of federal character rather than on the basis of national interest and as a result, we went from a fleet of 30 aircraft in 1982 to bankruptcy and a debt of over $60 million by 2000! In rebuilding Nigeria and positioning her for life without oil, which is a matter of when, not if, Nigeria must slay the monster of ethnicity and promote merit as the only yardstick for the management of her economy.

Recently I asked a question on Twitter. I tweeted 'How can youths be loyal to a country where their cut off mark in JAMB and Common Entrance depends on their state not their intelligence'? I also tweeted another question thus 'How do you explain to your child that his cut off mark for Common Entrance Exam is 65 while that of the neighbour's child is 7'? That by the way is a true story!

If you go to the Wikipedia page for Nigeria Airways, it shamefully says that "corruption and mismanagement" killed Nigeria Airways. Why won't corruption thrive in an environment where upward mobility depends on your state of origin rather than your state of intelligence? Why won't mismanagement thrive in a nation where you are from rather than take pre-eminence over what you know?

Recently, I was reading about a Nigerian who was running a major government agency in America and doing such a good job and my sadness was that I know for a fact that if this fellow had been in Nigeria, he was very unlikely to rise very far because he is from an area that is considered educationally advanced and would have to struggle to get the few positions zoned to his geo-political area. This is the real reason I condemned those accusing President Muhammadu Buhari of not balancing the appointments he has made so far, in that they complain that an overwhelming majority of his appointees are from the North. I condemned that argument on Twitter and a few people called me a betrayer, saying that as a Southerner, I should not have such a mindset.

My traducers fail to realise that they are making the wrong arguments. Where those appointees are from should not be the argument. The argument should be whether or not they are the best Nigeria has to offer. If they are the best we have to offer in terms of merit, then it does not matter to me if President Buhari appoints all his appointees from one village. Nigeria must make progress "though tribe and tongue may differ" and the only way we can do that is by saying bye to ethnicity and hello to merit. Until we do that, our development goals will remain a pipe dream.

My name is Ben Murray Bruce and I just want to make common sense.

Published: 8th September 2015

CHAPTER 3
BUILDING ENTREPRENEURSHIP:
LESSONS FROM GHANA

My heart was really burdened this past week by the news from the International Institute of Tropical Agriculture (IITA) that Ghana has overtaken Nigeria as the world's largest exporter of yams. Nigeria has a larger population than Ghana, along with a larger landmass of which a substantial part is very arable. So why is Ghana, with less human and material resources, overtaking us, with more human and material resources? According to Dr. Nobert Maroya, IITA's Project Manager for its Yam Improvement for Income and Food Security in West Africa project, the reason Ghana has overtaken Nigeria is because Ghana is more organised.

If I was tempted to doubt Dr. Maroya, my doubts disappeared when I saw a comment by a Nigerian to the story when it appeared on nairaland.com. A certain Oleri Smith commented thus "Don't mind those IITA people, what is IITA doing to put Nigeria back into exporting yam." I was taken aback by such a comment, but on second thought, I should have seen it coming. There is such a loss of responsibility in Nigeria that Nigerians, old and young, are very eager to cast blame on others for things that should be their responsibility.

IITA is a non-profit organisation set up by well meaning foreign institutions with the aim of helping African nations increase their capacity to feed themselves and yet we have Nigerians getting angry at them for a challenge that is not their fault and for which they are trying to render assistance. Talk about looking a gift horse in the mouth! What is it about Nigeria that we seem to be losing out in areas in which God in His infinite wisdom has given us ability and resources?

Just like yam, 50 years ago, Nigeria was the world's leading exporter of palm oil and then Malaysia sent experts to Nigeria to learn about our palm oil industry. Those experts returned to Malaysia with seedlings from Nigerian palm oil trees and in less than 20 years they overtook Nigeria and became the world's largest exporter of the product before being overtaken by Indonesia. We used to be one of the world's largest exporters of cocoa in the glorious days of Chief Obafemi Awolowo's Western Region. Today we have regressed and are not even among the top three importers of the product.

Even with crude oil, which brought us quick money and which many have blamed for making us lazy and dependent, we have also displayed this trait of mismanaging our competitive advantage over our competitors. Nigeria used to comfortably be the largest crude exporter in the African continent, but various experts have opined that Angola would overtake Nigeria as Africa's largest oil exporter next year. Some experts have pointed out that Angola has already overtaken Nigeria. Why do we seem to be losing ground on so many fronts?

I think the answer lies in the fact that our peculiar type of federation attunes us to think of revenue sharing rather than revenue generation. So, as our focus is on sharing whatever revenue we have, no one is interested in generating revenue and the few people who have a mindset of generating revenue are not encouraged to do so because no one wants to generate revenue for greedy and lazy leaders to share.

While our leaders have a "give me, give me, give me, my name is Jimmy" mentality, they forget that givers never lack because they have a production mentality but takers always need because they have a consumption mentality. We have a Revenue Mobilisation Allocation and Fiscal Commission (RMAFC) and a Federation Account Allocation Committee (FAAC) which are two of the most active bodies in Nigeria which are always in the news because we are obsessed with consumption and sharing. Where is the Revenue Generation Commission, where is the Federal Account Requisition Committee? Nigeria has reached a stage in which no one wants to produce but everyone wants to consume and we must change this or we will continue to lose grounds to smaller African nations.

And the way to change this is to start with our youth. We must train up a new generation of Nigerian youth who have a productive mindset and not a consumptive one. Have you noticed, for instance, that all our youths ever think of doing once they graduate from university is to look for a good job? If everybody wants a job and nobody wants to start a business, then who is going to be working for who? We cannot build a nation with only white-collar citizens? We need entrepreneurs, artisans, blue collar workers. What we have now is just a craze for paper qualifications so that we can acquire jobs and sit in an office as employees. Nations do not grow like that. And this is the main reason why employers are discriminating between degree holders and Higher National Diploma (HND) holders.

The original idea was that universities would be the institutions that would produce professionals like doctors, lawyers, engineers and architects who would, as entrepreneurs, go on to set up shop in their various professions, and that polytechnics would be the institutions that produce vocational and technical people who would set up small and medium scale enterprises. Graduates of the social sciences and the arts were to gravitate into the civil service and the Ivy League, while those from technical institutes would be the artisans and in that way society was to function without gaps.

But with the way our society has gravitated towards the worship of paper qualification, all these ideas which were in the Second National Development Plan of the Gowon administration were jettisoned and everyone did what was right in their own eyes until we have come to this sorry state where engineers sit in the Federal Ministry of Works undertaking purely administrative tasks and all the work has to be contracted to Julius Berger who has to fly in technical staff from Germany because there is a dearth of qualified technicians in Nigeria.

Such is the degeneration in Nigeria that if you need builders, electricians, tailors and other skilled artisans, you are better off hiring citizens from Nigeria's neighbouring nations! Even worse is our agricultural industry.

Our banks prefer to provide capital to fund consumption rather than production which is why they will lend to a business or individual that wants to import foods such as powdered milk, processed beef, tooth picks and fisheries which can be sold quickly and profitably, rather than a business or individual who wants to set up a farm or an agro-based industry. Going back to yam, Nigerians who used to love pounded yam now eat poundo yam (yam flour) and I was surprised to find that many elite Nigerians prefer to eat imported poundo rather than locally made ones. Our elite who grew up on pap, ogi and eko, would now not touch any porridge except it's Quaker oats.

As a child, I ate Nasco corn flakes and it was delicious and nutritious and most of all it was made in Nigeria. Today, our elite will not touch cornflakes except it is Kellogs! I have been to Ghana, which has now overtaken us in yam exports, and I see the patriotism in that nation which is lacking in Nigeria. If you are in Ghana, one of your first culture shocks would be that a large proportion of Ghanaians wear made in Ghana textiles which they will stylishly sew into the latest styles from the West. You see men with suits made out of ankara (local textile also known as wrapper, the kind made popular by Dr. Ngozi Okonjo-Iweala) or kente (a popular Ghanaian traditional fabric.) Their women even make tights and spaghetti dresses out of ankara!

It is clear that Ghanaians have adopted Western culture and modified it to suit their conditions and environment. They produce a lot of what they consume and are exporting the excess. This is why their institutions of learning now attract elite Nigerian families who send their children to secondary schools and universities in Ghana. As at 2014, there were over 75,000 Nigerians studying in Ghana after paying collective school fees of over $1 billion.

Education in Ghana is geared towards building entrepreneurs and the nation has a Ghana Entrepreneurs Foundation and has placed such a premium on entrepreneurship that they have a Ghana Entrepreneurs Hall of Fame into which they induct the most active entrepreneurs every year.

In a study published by the European Journal of Business and Management, it was revealed that over 23 per cent of Ghanaian university students have entrepreneurship inclination. And it is not just in yam that Ghana is dominating. In 2014, Ghana exported over 42,000 tonnes of vegetables to Europe. Ghanaian banks, on the prompting of the Ghanaian government, are lending huge funds to vegetable farmers which has enabled them to increase their yield and quality. Many Nigerians are unaware that Ghana's economy is growing faster than Nigeria's and climaxed at an exponential 15 per cent growth in 2011 and a projected 8 per cent growth in 2014.

In 1981, we asked Ghanians to leave Nigeria in the popular 'Ghana must go purge'. Yes, the Ghanaians left Nigeria. They did not just leave, they left Nigeria behind. So, what are the lessons Nigerian can learn from Ghana? The first and most important lesson is that we must shift our focus from revenue allocation to revenue generation. Just like Nigeria, Ghana has a revenue agency called the Ghana Revenue Authority (GRA), but unlike its Nigerian counterpart, the GRA is tasked with generating revenue for Ghana. We need to have a sober reflection on that in Nigeria.

Another lesson we can learn from Ghana is to reorder our education sector where we are not so focused on paper qualification only but are producing entrepreneurs, civil servants and skilled technicians who can staff our service industry. This will have the long term effect of overhauling our economy and moving it from a consumptive to a productive pattern.

But most importantly, we must put machinery in motion to revamp those industries in which we previously had comparative advantage. If at one point we were the world's leading exporters of palm oil, yam and groundnut, we can build our capacity to come back to the top again. We have the people and the land. What we need is the will.

My name is Ben Murray Bruce and I just want to make common sense.
Published: 26th October, 2015.

Chapter 4
My Advice to President Buhari
and his Team

Now that President Muhammadu Buhari has selected his 36 wise men, it would appear that the direction of his administration would become clearer. I had entertained some concerns about the delay in putting together a team especially after JP Morgan had announced in September that it would drop Nigeria from its emerging market bond index which immediately had a negative ripple effect on the economy. I know I was not the only one concerned. As an employer of labour with a thousand staff whose salaries I must pay, I know that not a few of my employees and fellow employers of labour expressed similar concerns especially as Barclays indicated that it was soon to follow the route taken by JP Morgan.

However, with a cabinet about to be in place, it is the expectation of Nigerians and the international community that the concerns raised by international banking consortiums and global rating agencies on Nigeria's economic direction would soon be addressed. Yet, now is the time for well meaning Nigerians to speak up and articulate ideas to the president and his ministerial nominees on what steps they could take to improve their chances of success at turning around Nigeria. I have always believed that it is the height of mental laziness to reject ideas because they come from an All Progressives Congress (APC) or Peoples Democratic Party (PDP) person. That type of behaviour ushers in silly season in politics and business.

I mean, Nigeria's economy is tanking. Our economy could even be said to be sick. Anybody that fails to see this may be living in denial. Does a sick man reject the cure for his sickness because his doctor is PDP or APC? I think not. So I urge the government and the party in power to have an ear to the ground and soup up advice. Who knows where the solution to our economic situation will come from? On my own part, I would offer some advice to the president and his would-be cabinet on little things that they can do to build a better working relationship amongst themselves and between them and the Nigerian people. My advice may be small, but I would urge my readers not to underestimate the big difference small changes make.

My first advice is to the would-be cabinet of which I played a part in their successful screening in the Senate of the National Assembly last week. Each of them, no matter what portfolio they are eventually given, must see their job as COMPLEMENTING each other as part of a complementary team and not as COMPETING with each other as individual runners in a race. I have been up close and personal to almost all administrations in Nigeria beginning from my tutelage under Vice-Admiral Akinwale Wey who taught me much of what I know of Nigerian history and our style of government to my mentoring under the sagacious intellectual, President Olusegun Obasanjo.

If the public knew how much of the failure of successive administration was caused by infighting and competition amongst ministers and kitchen cabinet members they would actually stop blaming past presidents and heads of state and direct their verbal missiles at their aides. Competition within an administration distracts the president and impedes the ability of the government to deliver the goods.

In the last 16 years of civil rule, Nigerians have witnessed the rise of online news sites that have become a thorn in the flesh of governments at all levels because of the sensitive news, half truths and down right lies they sensationally publish. Nothing has distracted Nigerian governments over the years as these news outlets. They have also been assisted by print tabloids that call themselves news magazines but which publish sleaze instead of mainstream news. I can authoritatively state that much of the sensitive news that finds its way to these media emanate from competing ministers and infighting kitchen cabinet members struggling to outdo each other by secretly revealing embarrassing information about their colleagues to undermine their influence with the president.

Where they have no dirty laundry to air against their colleagues, they cook up lies and half truths and these websites, hungry for Internet traffic, and their print media colleagues desperate to increase circulation and advertising, publish these stories without verification which are then swallowed by an unwitting public hook, line and sinker. The end result is that the government starts to react and once a government enters reaction mode, the administration loses the moral authority it requires in order to achieve anything meaningful and must from that time rely on authority borrowed from the offices its members occupy.

Let me ask President Buhari if he can remember the names of President Abraham Lincoln's aides and cabinet members. I am even going too far. No one remembers who served with Ronald Reagan. They only remember Reagan and Bush!

For President Buhari to be successful, he must not tolerate the type of self-defeating behaviour I outlined above because while his ministers will share in his success, none of them will share in his failure. If the administration fails, history will record that Buhari failed.

He is best served if he reminds his ministers that there is no 'I' in team work and as such individual team members must resist the urge to use the media to promote themselves. Let their work promote them instead. No matter what individual cabinet members in any government may think, none of them is as smart as all of them, therefore it is their teamwork that will make the president's dream work!

It has been rightly said that if you see yourself as the big picture, your reflection will prevent you from seeing the true big picture. And if I may ask, what is the true big picture? That is a question that can only be answered by President Buhari as he makes his vision so clear to his team because if a leader has no vision his team has failed before they even began. Change is a slogan not a vision!

My next advice to President Buhari is that he must live out the adage he articulated during his Independence Day broadcast when he said that "order is more vital than speed". His ministers would be in a hurry to impress him. Many of them who themselves have presidential or gubernatorial ambitions would be in a hurry to impress Nigerians. As such, they may bind the government by making wild but popular promises in order to ingratiate themselves into the good books of the president and the public. But such behaviour is counter productive because though the windmills of government surely, they also grind slowly. Very slowly.

Nigerians have not so soon forgotten ministers who promised them uninterrupted power supply by year's end. Years have passed since those promises were made and either the ministers meant light years or the light they referred to was candle light! You see, when you are in government, you should not be in a hurry because people will forget how fast you did the job but they will not forget how good or bad you did it! Then moving on to the president, I sincerely advise him to value his ministers because cabinet members work for the vision of a president that values them and sabotage the agenda of presidents that they feel do not value them.

Although what I am about to say may raise unpleasant memories in the president, but his own personal history bears out the truth of what I have said immediately above. He should be tolerant to his ministers and ensure that he talks to them or with them but never at them!

If any of them habitually comes to him with juicy gossip on other team members (as would undoubtedly happen), he should save his administration by showing such a one the door. As soon as he does that, all other ministers will fall in line!

Finally, President Buhari should remember that leadership is pure and simply the ability to translate vision to reality. He should use that as a yardstick for deciding who remains in the cabinet and who gets dropped. Ministers must deliver results and not activity. The president ran on an agenda of change. His ministers must make change a reality or jump off the change trains with alacrity.

These are my little nuggets of advice to the president. I give this advice not because I am a supporter of the president or his party but because I am a supporter of Nigeria and it is in my interest that the driver of the car called Nigeria, in which I am a passenger, gets the car to its destination safely and with the passengers in good condition to continue the journey that goes on and on.

My name is Ben Murray Bruce and I just want to make common sense!
Published: 21st October, 2015.

CHAPTER 5
HID AWOLOWO: THE LABOURS OF OUR HEROES' PAST SHALL NEVER BE IN VAIN

Last week, I was at the Ikenne home of the Awolowo's to condole with the family on the death of the matriarch, Chief (Mrs) Hannah Idowu Dideolu Awolowo. Let me rephrase that. I thought I was going to condole with the family, but when I got to Ikenne, I found out that I was actually there to celebrate not just mama, but her husband, Chief Obafemi Jeremiah Oyeniyi Awolowo, their dynasty and the Black Race. What I saw first hand at Ikenne proved to me that the Awolowo's do not need our eulogies and kind words. The exemplary lives lived by mama HID and her husband, the sage, already eulogised them!

At Ikenne, I was taken to a huge library in the premises that was filled with books. To my pleasant surprise, Chief Awolowo's granddaughter, who gave me the tour, told me that her grand father had read each and every book in that library! As she told me that, I began to be inspired. That one man had read all those books was a triumph! That that man never became president of Nigeria was a disaster! He would have been Nigeria's Philosopher king!

I was showed Chief Awolowo's Holy Bible, which was well worn. Then I was shown his Qur'an and it was equally evident that the owner of that sacred book had thumped through it with purpose.

Today, Nigeria is going through the most radical and extreme form of religious intolerance from both sides of the great Abrahamic faiths that dominate Nigeria, Christianity and Islam.

Can you imagine the level of religious tolerance that would have been our reality today if a man who had understanding of the origins, morals, ethos and philosophy that permeate the two great Abrahamic faiths had ruled Nigeria! That journey that I thought was a condolence visit soon turned into a odyssey into the world of two people who loved each other and whose lives were so intertwined and connected to the purpose of uplifting the Black Race.

Many people erroneously think that mama HID was just a consort to Chief Awolowo who played a spectator role while he made history. Nothing could be further than the truth!

This woman, who Chief Awolowo called his "jewel of inestimable value", proved that that praise was not empty when she carried on the battle for him when he was imprisoned by the Balewa government during which time she spearheaded the merger between the Action Group (AG) and the National Council of Nigeria and the Cameroons (NCNC), which led to the emergence of the United Progressive Grand Alliance (UPGA), which was the precursor of today's All Progressive Congress (APC).

I saw her pictures as a young lady and mama was a paragon of beauty, however, she was no trophy wife. She was a wife of destiny to her husband as she modelled the behaviour of the virtuous woman described in Proverbs 31 by raising an outstanding family and being very active in business to the point that she built an empire based on thrift and submitted the same to her husband. It was famously said by the late Dim Emeka Odumegwu Ojukwu that Chief Awolowo was the best president we never had. Let me add that mama HID Awolowo was the best First Lady we never had. While I was at Ikenne, I saw people come in and heard people calling to pour encomiums on mama and her husband.

The see encomiums are nice, however, what this dynamic duo need now is a preservation of their legacy. Not enough Nigerian youths know what this couple of destiny did for their parents and their nation. The duo of Chief Awolowo and mama HID are our own version of Dr. Martin Luther King and Coretta Scott King. Because of what they achieved, millions of children in the Western Region of Nigeria went to school without paying a dime and have gone on to live meaningful lives that have added value to the world. This year, Scotland Yard and the Metropolitan Police announced that they were looking to hire Yoruba speaking officers to join the force in London.

Why are they doing this? Why are they not looking to employ Swahili speaking cops? Why are they not looking to employ Afrikaans speaking cops? Why are they not looking to employ even cops that speak a European language, like Russian? They are taking this unique step, because a huge proportion of the population of Greater London are Nigerians who speak Yoruba. And not only are they large in number, they are educated and landed and own some of the choicest properties in London. Included in their number was the recently departed Antonio Deinde Fernandez and Adebayo Ogunlesi, Chairman and Managing Partner of Global Infrastructure Partners, which owns Gatwick Airport and other choice property all over London, The UK and the world.

When you begin to trace the timelines of when Nigerians and particularly Yoruba speakers started their ascendancy in the UK and the rest of the world, you will find that it started in 1955 after the Western Region Government of Nigeria headed by Chief Awolowo initiated free education in Western Nigeria. Now that they papa and mama are both gone, it is time for Nigeria and the men and women who benefited from their visionary leadership to preserve their legacy. How you may ask? There are a variety of ways to preserve their legacy. As I sit here typing, the image of Chief Awolowo's library continues to flash in my mind and a good place to start will be by getting the Federal Government of Nigeria to push for that library to be declared a World Heritage Site by the United Nations Educational, Scientific and Cultural Organisation (UNESCO).

If the federal government initiates the process, it will be successful and will cement Chief Awolowo and HID Awolowo's image in the world's memory. Concurrently, the federal government should declare the library as a National Heritage site. Also, the states that now comprise the former Western Region of Nigeria could consider instituting a fund for the preservation of the ideals the Awolowo's stood for.

Individuals of means, particularly from the Western Region, should be invited to contribute to such a fund. I am sure if the six states of the former Western Region along with the two states that came out of the Mid West Region (Edo and Delta) constitute a committee for such a purpose, then individuals like Mike Adenuga, Adebayo Ogunlesi, Femi Otedola and Mrs. Folorunsho Alakija will be willing, even eager to contribute to it. It is a worthy cause. The monies from such a fund could then be managed by the Obafemi Awolowo Foundation to be used to advance the legacy of the late sage and his wife through whatever vehicle they deem fit.

Nollywood should not also be left out. Industry veterans should produce documentaries or biographies of Chief Awolowo for our youths to watch so that they know what the man did to plant trees whose shades they are now enjoying. When such movies or documentaries are made, I make a solemn promise to air it repeatedly on Silverbird Television for free. I also covenant that all Silverbird Cinemas will show it for free to members of the public. Come on guys, we have to promote and preserve our own if not their memory will die! Nigeria's founding fathers were Sir Ahmadu Bello, Owelle Nnamdi Azikiwe and Chief Awolowo.

Today all three are dead but what do our youth know about them? Virtually nothing!

Our youths know about John F Kennedy, Nelson Mandela, Mungo Park, David Livingstone and even oppressors like Cecil Rhodes but they do not know about our founding fathers.

One of the first history lessons all American children learn about is the founding fathers. They learn about who they were, what they did and what route they took to getting to their enviable heights in society. There is even a larger than life national monument carved into the face of a mountain to commemorate the founding fathers at Mount Rushmore in South Dakota.

Nations like America take the pains to commemorate their founding fathers and other important heroes in order not to forget their national purpose and their collective vision.

If they do not do this, in time their memories will fade away and they will not be accurately represented in contemporary life.

A good example of this is Chief Moshood Abiola. When Abiola died on July 7 1998, students of the University of Lagos shut down Akoka in Lagos and insisted that Nigeria must immortalise Abiola. They stopped motorists and made them chant anti federal government slogans and pro Abiola messages. Fast forward to May 29, 2012 when former President Goodluck Jonathan renamed the University of Lagos the Moshood Abiola University of Lagos. On that day, it was the students of the University of Lagos, whose predecessors once demanded that the federal government immortalise Abiola, that trooped out in large numbers to condemn the renaming of their institution after Abiola. So intense was this demonstration that the University of Lagos had to be shut down the next day on May 30th 2012. What had happened in the intervening years to douse the enthusiasm of the students over the immortalisation of Abiola?

You see, because the government and the larger society did not make enough conscious effort to remember Abiola's legacy by teaching it to our youth, our youth forgot and with the passage of time the memory became dimmer and dimmer. Yet this very Abiola once donated a fortune to the University of Lagos and sponsored many events and activities in that institution. We cannot afford to fulfil the derisive slur of racists that if you want to hide anything from a Black man you do it by putting it in a book! We must capture the legacy of not just our founding fathers but also our national heroes in books, films, buildings, holidays and monuments.

Chief Awolowo's contemporary, Owelle Azikiwe, died on the 11th of May 1996. Till today, the federal government has yet to fulfil its pledge to complete a mausoleum for him. Nigerians do not even know what Azikiwe's wife's name was and if not that we had a president whose middle name is Azikiwe, the memory of the great Zik of Africa was almost fading away from our political life.

By contrast, Baroness Margaret Thatcher died on the 8th of April 2013, yet even before her death, the British Government consulted her on how she would like to be buried and remembered in the event of her death and ultimately spent £3.6 million of tax payers funds for that purpose. Two years before she died, Hollywood made a $13 million biography about her entitled The Iron Lady to capture her legacy. So good was the movie that Meryl Streep, who played Mrs. Thatcher, received an Oscar for her portrayal of Baroness Thatcher. Since her death, Parliament, 10 Downing Street and various British institutions have preserved her legacy by building institutions and endowing centres to study her ideas and philosophy. Only on July 13 this year (2015), her successor, Prime Minister David Cameron, unveiled the Thatcher Business Education Centre.

More than 100 books have been written about the life, legacy and personality of Thatcher and it is safe to say that she would never be forgotten. Now let us compare the remembrance given to Azikiwe to that given to Thatcher and we will understand why Britain, a country with only a third of our population, wields more influence than us on the world stage. When we do not value our own heroes, we are communicating to the world that we do not value ourselves. I mean who would want to be the hero of a people that according to the late Bob Marley, "kill their prophets"?

We were all in Nigeria pretending that someone like Fela was not a prophet. It took two Americans, Billy T Jones and Jim Lewis, to write the book

Fela! It also took three Americans, Jay Z with Will Smith and his wife, Jada Pinkett, to bring the book to life on Broadway, and an American, Sahr Ngaujah, was cast as Fela. All because we do not value our prophets!

I guess all I am trying to say is that the value of each individual Nigerian is tied to the value we attach to our founding fathers and other heroes who sacrificed for us to get to where we are.

You cannot divorce yourself from Nigeria. Even if you immigrate, change your name and pick up a new accent, it will still come out that you are a Nigerian. That being the case should we not learn to like being Nigerians and teach the world to like Nigerians? In achieving this, we must borrow a verse from the George Benson song made popular by Whitney Houston, 'The Greatest Love of All'. A verse in that song goes 'Learning to love yourself. It is the greatest love of all'. What an awesome message to Nigeria and Nigerians.

In conclusion, I beg Nigerians. We should not just gather and spend billions to throw a big owambe party in honour of mama HID Awolowo as she is buried. All the champagne, meat, rice, pounded yam and soup we will eat, plus the aso ebi we will purchase, will not last. We will either pass them away or the cloth will fade after washing. But if we document her and papa's life, the document will last and help us produce modern day Awolowos who can take us to our Promised Land. And God knows we need them!

My name is Ben Murray Bruce and I just want to make common sense!
Published: 28th September, 2015.

CHAPTER 6
OF NIGERIA, MANDELA AND REGGAE MUSIC

I am former President Goodluck Jonathan's senator. He is my constituent in the Bayelsa East senatorial zone that I represent in the Senate of the National Assembly and I am sufficiently aware of what he did and did not do while he was president of Nigeria. Former President Jonathan achieved a lot of things for Nigeria during his term and I think it is a revision of history for anyone or institution to propagate the narrative that he set Nigeria back. How could that be the case when under him Nigeria became the leading economy in Africa and our average life expectancy grew from 47 years to 51.7 years which represents the single largest increase in our annals? Thankfully, these records, especially the one for the increase in life expectancy come from no less a body than the United Nations, so no one can say that Jonathan manipulated these records.

It is not that I have set out to defend Jonathan in this piece, but I think someone has to be responsible enough to say that Jonathan is out of the picture and to continue to blame him and his administration for Nigeria's current problems betrays a defeatist mentality by those who are engaging in that pastime. This 'blame it all on Jonathan' song can sustain those who sing it in the short term, but eventually it will work in Jonathan's favour. Those in the frontline of the anti-Jonathan chorus are more responsible than anybody else for keeping Jonathan in the consciousness of Nigerians which cannot be good for the present administration.

When you are out of political office, your greatest need shifts from the need to be seen as performing to the need for relevance. It is the government in power that needs to perform. Everybody else only needs to be relevant. And Jonathan's enemies are making him relevant.

In fact, by blaming Jonathan for all of Nigeria's problems, his enemies make him the main issue in Nigerian politics which is good for him and not for them.

Let me use an analogy here. In the 80s, reggae music was at the zenith of its popularity and all over the world, from the Caribbean, to Europe to Africa, reggae musicians were singing mostly one song. All their songs centred around freeing Nelson Mandela. However, when Mandela was unexpectedly released in 1991, the popularity of reggae music nosedived because reggae musicians had lost their number one source of inspiration! So, while Mandela went on to become the most relevant black man of his lifetime, those that sang about his release gradually faded away into obscurity.

Are we seeing a replay of this scenario in Nigeria? Instead of all this Jonathan bashing, should we not be more concerned about the clear and present dangers facing this nation?

For instance, Nigeria has the fastest growing population in the world. While the population of Europe is projected to shrink by 2050, Nigeria's population is expected to surpass that of the United States and by 2100 it is projected that we will rival China's population. Yet, as the population of Nigeria is exploding right before our eyes, some people are talking about dismantling the Jonathan era policies that were actually preparing us for the dramatic increase in our population without themselves coming up with alternative solutions. The new song is to jettison the National Conference report which made progressive suggestions on how to make our economy and polity less dependent on oil which is a diminishing resource.

The agricultural policies of Akinwumi Adesina while he was minister of agriculture are being pooh poohed for political reasons instead of celebrating and continuing with them. The man led changes that reduced our food import bill by over $4 billion and increased our ability to feed ourselves yet we do not want to recognise that because it is a fruit from the Jonathan tree.

The Jonathan administration weeded out 50,000 ghost workers from the federal civil service through the introduction and strict compliance with the Integrated Payroll and Personnel Information System (IPPIS), yet instead of applauding Dr. (Mrs.) Ngozi Okonjo-Iweala for this feat, we are instead bailing out states that cannot pay workers' salaries precisely because many of those workers are ghost workers! Tell me who will feed us in 2050 when we have more mouths to feed than the entire populations of those countries to whom we would be looking for help? Jonathan was building schools for Almajiris and there are those insulting him for that and calling it a misplaced priority forgetting that if we do not educate the 10 million out-of-school children that the United Nations estimate exists in Northern Nigeria, a day will come when the population of out-of-school Nigerian children will be more than in-school children and the resultant effect on our national security will be nothing short of catastrophe!

Nigeria's politics has to mature. We have to realise that once elections are over, we must all accept the outcome and learn to work with each other. It is a big, big misconception that you have to like people to work with them or to build upon what they started. If man had kept reinventing the wheel, we would never have invented the plane. Every generation must build upon where the previous generation stopped from. That is the story of human progress since the fall of man in Eden to the Internet age of today. If Alexander Graham Bell did not invent the telephone, we would not have the Internet today. If we had complained about the complication associated with the land line and jettisoned the idea of a telephone, we would not have made progress in telephony to the point where we have mobile phones! If every new administration keeps starting from the scratch and wastes its honeymoon period demonising its predecessor, both Nigeria and the administration may find it difficult to fulfil their potential.

Enough of this rear view mirror focus we have been regaled with these past few months. It is time to man up and take responsibility for the way things are and take action to make progress. Thankfully, not everyone has been caught up in the 'blame it all on Jonathan' frenzy. Of all the present office holders, the only person that seems to have come to grips with the economic reality Nigeria finds itself in is the current Governor of the Central Bank of Nigeria (CBN) Godwin Emefiele. His idea of introducing home grown pragmatic policies to curtail what we spend our foreign exchange on is the only saving grace that has kept the naira at the level it is in.

If not for Emefiele's decision to stop the sale of foreign exchange for the importation of 40 items, we would have been experiencing perhaps a rate of 500 to $1. By this action, Emefiele has shut out those who previously wasted our foreign exchange importing luxury or non-essential commodities such as toothpicks, glass and glassware, kitchen utensils, tables, textiles, woven fabrics, clothes, plastic and rubber products, soap and cosmetic, tomatoes/tomato paste, margarine, palm kernel/palm oil products/vegetable oil, meat and processed meat products, vegetable and processed vegetable products, poultry — chicken, eggs, turkey — private airplanes/jet and Indian incense. Can you imagine that the CBN had been subsidising the importation of toothpicks, wheel barrows and palm oil which are products that we can conveniently produce in Nigeria? Are we going to die if we do not import Indian incense? What is that even used for in the first place? Or that at a time Nigeria had become a net exporter of cement we were still allowing people to import cement with our scarce foreign exchange?

We have millions of youths looking for jobs yet we were allowing people import chicken and eggs instead of financing our small and medium scale enterprises to go into such ventures which will meet our needs while providing jobs for our youths. These are the types of things that deserve our attention and I thank God Nigeria has people like Emefiele who has not allowed himself to be distracted by all the Jonathan bashing such that he is providing a steady hand at a time when other hands are unsteady. Hopefully, those engaged in this conduct will come back to reality and stop their blame-shifting dance. If there is ever any man to blame for your present condition, it is never the man that sat in the seat you now seat on. It is always the man in the mirror!

My name is Ben Murray Bruce and I just want to make common sense!
Published: 18th September, 2015.

Chapter 7
Taking a Mercedes Benz 450SEL for Service

Most Nigerians have come to accept that the Nigerian National Petroleum Corporation (NNPC) must perform Turn Around Maintenance (TAM) on our refineries, but what we do not know is that the cost of these TAM is so high that it would actually make better sense to build a new refinery than to continue having these maintenances.

As an example, the cost for the TAM for the Port Harcourt refinery, as tendered by the original builder, was $297 million as of 2013. However, in the same year, the Azeri state energy company SOCAR built a 40,000 barrel per day refining capacity refinery at $250 million in Kyrgyzstan.

Also in the same year, Comico Oil built a 100,000 barrel per day refining capacity refinery for $250 million in Serbia. These are but a few examples of refineries being built with an amount less than what we spend on maintaining our own refinery.

Does this make sense especially when Nigeria's crude, the Bonny Light Sweet Crude, is very low in sulfur and easy to refine? Something is wrong somewhere!

If other nations are building refineries for the price it takes us to maintain our refineries, I posit that it is better for us to sell our present refineries and use the money we are currently devoting to TAM to build new refineries that will create jobs and reduce our dependency on foreign fuel.

All our refineries are old. The Port Harcourt refinery was built in 1965 and upgraded in 1989. The Warri refinery was built in 1978, while the Kaduna refinery was finished in 1980. Our refineries have an average age of over 30 years. Since they were built, new technology has been introduced that has made much of their operating systems near obsolete. This is the reason why we are spending colossal sums to maintain them.

To put things into perspective, imagine taking a Mercedes Benz 450SEL

6.9 for servicing at a Mercedes Benz authorised service agent in the year 2015. The service may cost you even more than the car is worth because Mercedes Benz stopped making the 450SEL in 1981. Any part required for the service would have to be custom made from Germany or cannibalised from another Mercedes Benz 450SEL. If the service agent will be truthful to you, the best advice would be to buy a new Mercedes because there is nothing as expensive as an old Mercedes.

This is the state in which Nigeria finds itself with her refineries. Our refineries are old and their technology has not been upgraded over the years. TAM is called Turn Around Maintenance for a reason. They are designed to maintain a refinery not upgrade it. China for instance has passed a Cleaner Production Promotion Law of the People's Republic of China, that will lead to "phasing out outmoded process units and technically transforming and improving older refineries".

In 1982, America had 301 refineries with a combined refining capacity of 17.9 million barrels. Today, America has reduced the number of her refineries by half by shutting down the old refineries and building newer, cheaper and more energy efficient refineries and they have maintained the same refining capacity! In other words, the US has reduced the size of her capacity by 50 per cent and maintained 100 per cent of her output by adopting new technology.

With new technologies that have simplified the process of desalting and fluid catalytic cracking, the business of refining has evolved. But rather than evolve, Nigeria continues to take her Mercedes Benz 450SEL to the dealership for service as usual. The dealers will happily take our money but that does not change the fact that technology has left us behind!

If illiterate and semi literate Nigerians in the Niger Delta are able to refine crude oil locally and come out with petrol that works in cars, doesn't that tell us that crude oil refining has been simplified enough to the point where it has become Do It Yourself! In 2014, the Nigerian Navy announced that it had destroyed over 260 illegal refineries in the Warri area alone! To me that is rather short sighted. Yes, what this people have done is wrong, but it is still evidence of local ingenuity.

What I think should have been done is that the Navy should have arrested these people and handed them over to the police. Thereafter, NNPC in conjunction with the Ministry of Justice, should offer them amnesty if they are willing to reveal the methods they used in refining crude into petroleum products. These methods should then be patented by the NNPC who may then wish to apply them (after tweaking it) for the establishment of inexpensive refineries in Nigeria. After all who cares how petrol is refined as long as it can fuel a car without damaging it? To paraphrase myself and Chairman Mao of China, "It doesn't matter whether a fuel is black or white, if it moves a car it is good fuel."

But then corrupt officials will not let this be. After all they allegedly make money by inflating contracts for the TAM of our refineries and as a result will not want the system to end. That is why we need to run NNPC in a businesslike manner. Right now, President Muhammadu Buhari simply appoints the group managing director (GMD) and board of the corporation. There are no strict rules regarding who may or may not be appointed as GMD and board member of the corporation.

The NNPC, which is a creation of statute, is more important to Nigeria than say a corporation like the Federal Inland Revenue Service (FIRS), yet, the president needs Senate confirmation to appoint the head of FIRS but not the GMD or board members of the NNPC. Does this make sense? If we ensure that the strictest recruitment criteria is followed in staffing, the NNPC from top to bottom and that at the top the recruitment is subject to Senate approval, we will have a brand new NNPC. Once you can get a new merit-based team in place and give them targets, Nigerians would be surprised how quickly the NNPC improves. Until then, all we are doing is taking our Mercedes Benz 450SEL for servicing.

My name is Ben Murray Bruce and I just want to make common sense!
Published: 14th September, 2015

Chapter 8
If You Build It People Will Come

One of the things that really riles me is when I receive complaints by foreigners and mostly Westerners about the difficulty in getting a visa to visit Nigeria. Not only is the process unnecessarily long and tedious, a Nigerian visa is also expensive and can cost as much as $200. For a nation that wants to diversify her revenue base, this is the wrong approach.

This constraint is also one of the reasons why Nigerian fares poorly in the annual Ease of Doing Business ranking list in the Global Competitive Index (GCI) published by the World Economic Forum.

Last year, Nigeria fell seven places to 127th position from the 120th position we occupied in 2013. Not much has changed to expect a better rating this year. And yet, we expect to be open for business! The first thing that foreigners look at in determining the ease of doing business in a country is how easy it is to enter and leave that nation. We have our work cut out for us.

If I may ask, what will a Westerner want to do in Nigeria if not business or touring? They are very unlikely to engage in crime and we have checks in place to ensure that they do not sabotage our economy. So why make them jump through hoops to get a visa when it is actually us that needs their business or presence as tourists? Nigeria needs to take a cue from the United Arab Emirates (UAE) and throw open her borders to business and pleasure seekers with the only requirement for entry being that you have money to spend in Nigeria.

Even if we need to place visa restrictions, we can do it for certain nations whose citizens will have a higher incentive to take advantage of our economy. We should not place the same conditions on everybody. That's crazy!

Recently, some missionaries from the United States wanted to visit Nigeria. They had plans to explore opening up schools or helping to staff schools that already exist. They also had plans to help Nigerian orphans get adopted by wealthy Americans. I am quite sad to say that the hoops put in their way discouraged them and eventually they did not actualise their plans. Instead of adopting from Nigeria, they ended up adopting Chinese.

This is not an isolated story. It keeps happening over and over again. I know of Westerners who wanted to set up a refinery in Nigeria and their attempts to get a visa where so tedious. Thank God they knew someone who knew the Ambassador in their country. Only then where things able to work out for them. But what about the ones that do not know anybody? Must you know someone to have your visa process fast tracked? This ought not to be so.

The world has evolved and although it is now cliche to say it, but we now live in a global village. Globalisation is the present and future of the world. Since the fall of the Berlin Wall in 1989, national borders have been falling and people now become world citizens instead of citizens of one nation. Westerners and Asians are now so wealthy and are looking for new places to invest or visit as tourists and nations like the UAE are visionary enough to see this new world order and are tapping into it.

By making her visa policy so lenient, the UAE has attracted the world's business and tourist visitors. As long as you have money to spend, their borders are open to you. And what has been the result? By opening up her borders to the world, the UAE's economy has more than doubled and though she is an oil rich nation, over 30 per cent of her Gross Domestic Product comes from her aviation industry. Between 10-12 per cent comes from the tourists industry. This is a total of over $180 billion per annum!

This amount would not have come into her economy if His Highness, Sheikh Mohammed bin Rashid Al Maktoum had not been visionary enough to open his nation's borders to the world for business and pleasure in the 1990s. We do not have to reinvent the wheel in Nigeria. We can just replicate what has been done successfully in Dubai. And it will be very shortsighted to say that foreigners will not visit Nigeria because of the crisis of terrorism we are currently going through.

The Mano River region had been war torn for decades starting from the late 80s, but that did not stop the growth of the tourist industry in the Republic of the Gambia. Gambia is one of those nations that liberalised its visa policy early enough and the result has been that tourism is the number one foreign exchange earner in that nation. What about Kenya? Tourism in Kenya is the second largest source of foreign exchange revenue following agriculture. Their annual revenue from tourism is just a little over $1 billion per annum. Yet, this is a country that is grappling with terrorism just as we are. Kenya has a very liberal visa policy that is raking in dollars for her economy.

To put things into perspective, tourism is to Gambia and Kenya what oil is to Nigeria. To put things into even more perspective, oil is not a renewable resource. It has a shelf life. It will finish one day or lose value sooner than that. But tourism is a renewable resource. It will always exists. As an economic mainstay, it is safer than oil! Americans have a saying which is true. They say, if you build it, people will come. If Nigeria builds up her capacity to host the world, the world will come! A good place to start would be by liberalising our visa policy. Let us make it easy for people to visit Nigeria. This will have the effect of increasing travel to Nigeria and our aviation industry will boom!

We have Bilateral Air Service Agreements (BASA) with many nations but we are not utilising them. However, those nations are utilising theirs and Nigerians are trooping to their countries to spend dollars. By now, it is almost a notorious fact that the Lagos-London-Lagos route is perhaps the most profitable route in the would for British Airways because Nigerians are trooping to the United Kingdom for holidays. Why can't we flip that? The reverse is the case for Gambia. 50,000 British tourists visit The Gambia every year.

The United Kingdom is not making money from The Gambia, it is The Gambia that is making money from them which is as it should be!

Turkey has now liberalised her visa policy such that if you have a British or American visa you do not need a Turkish visa to enter Turkey as long as you fly Turkish Airlines! Do you know how many billions of dollars Turkey has reaped by that policy? People will come to Nigeria. We must believe in ourselves and in our economy. And that brings me to business registration. We must make it easy to register a business in Nigeria. Currently it is too difficult and expensive to open a business in Nigeria.

Registering a company with the Corporate Affairs Commission (CAC) can cost up to N60,000 and takes weeks to finalise. Meanwhile in the US you can register a business in a day with less than $50 and you do not have to leave your house! We must make if easy for people to open business in Nigeria. We must also make it easier for business to open accounts in Nigerian banks. We must never underestimate the big difference small changes can make. These are small changes that are within our power to make and if we make them we will be stunned at the positive multiplier effect they will cause.

My name is Ben Murray Bruce and I just want to make common sense!
Published: 17th August, 2015.

Chapter 9
Integrating the Fulani into Modern Day Nigeria

It will shock Nigerians to know that more people have died as a result of Fulani/indigene clashes in the last half a decade than have died from terrorist activity occasioned by the Boko Haram terrorist sect. As horrific as individual Boko Haram activities are, they pale in comparison to the barbarous slaughter of over 500 men, women, and children in a single night of terror at Dogo na Hauwa village of Plateau State of 2010.

Terrorist activities occasioned by the Boko Haram terrorist group have been largely localised in Nigeria's North-east save for some sporadic attacks in other parts of the North and the Federal Capital Territory.

However, Fulani/indigene clashes have occurred in every state of Nigeria bar none! Needless lives have been lost all over Nigeria in these clashes and this will continue in perpetuity if as a nation we do not take steps to change the conditions that give rise to these clashes.

Just as with the Romany Gypsies of Europe, it is very easy to blame this itinerant group of cattle herders, buying such an exercise would in my opinion be an exercise in futility. I share the same view as movie producer, J. Michael Straczynski, who famously said: "People spend too much time finding other people to blame, too much energy finding excuses for not being what they are capable of being, and not enough energy putting themselves on the line, growing out of the past, and getting on with their lives." Nigeria must grow out of her past and that cannot happen until Nigerians stop pointing in blame and starting pointing to solutions.

Even before there was a nation called Nigeria, the Fulani had been passing through several nations en route markets all over West Africa. Year in and year out, they followed established grazing routes and as long as their cattle had grass and vegetation to feed on, they coexisted in peace with communities along their grazing routes. But as West Africa became increasingly urbanised, it was and is a matter of time before increase in population put pressure on local communities to use the ancient Fulani grazing routes for farmland or residential purposes.

It is the competition for the scarce commodity of land that has brought about friction between the Fulani's and the indigenous people along these reserves. So what do we do? What is the solution? Obviously we cannot do nothing and watch as people continue to die all over Nigeria.

We must do something and I propose that Nigeria should take the following series of steps.

We should restore the ancient grazing routes of Fulani pastoralists. Both the Federal Ministry of Agriculture and the Federal Ministry of Lands should work with the apex Fulani pastoral association, the Miyetti Allah Cattle Breeders Association, to revive these routes and where there have been farms or houses built on these routes, alternative routes must be found.

Next, the Federal Ministry of Agriculture should give a deadline of no less than 10 years to the Miyetti Allah Cattle Breeders Association to convert from pastoral cattle rearing to the modern business of cattle ranching in which cattle are reserved, reared and bred at a central location suitable for such purposes.

Measurable timelines should be agreed with the Miyetti Allah Cattle Breeders Association for progress towards this objective and penalties for failure to progress towards these timelines must be clearly spelt out.

Next, the Federal Ministries of Finance and Defence must collaborate through their agencies to monitor and ensure proper taxation of the informal cattle rearing economy and also to ensure that the government can trace the whereabouts of individual Fulani clans. This can be done easily by identifying the cattle rearers entry point into Nigeria and stationing mobile border posts there with armed officials of the Nigerian Customs Service Department of Animal Control.

Upon entry into Nigeria, every cattle must be shot with a homing device which will enable Customs officials and the ministry of defence track each cattle as they enter Nigeria and to pin point their location anywhere within our borders. These devices are cheap and practical.

There is a huge informal economy that is not taxed by the various governments in Nigeria. Tagging these cattle as they enter Nigerian soil will not just have positive security implications, it will also affect the economy positively as the federal government will have accurate numbers of the total cattle on the hoof that enters Nigeria and how much to charge as duty on each cattle.

By tagging the cattle, Nigeria will not only increase her revenue base in a world of falling oil prices, but we will have the additional benefit of knowing in real time where each herd of cattle are within our borders and how to proactively deploy our police and military for internal security issues to prevent Fulani/Indigene clashes. Nigeria has too many intellectuals who know how to analyse problems and give angles to them. But we do not have enough minds working on solutions. We will make more progress if our public intellectualism is geared towards solving than the analysis of challenges. Nations make more progress when their leaders are more concerned with accepting responsibility than with apportioning blame.

This is the mindset to solving the Fulani/indigene and all other similar and related incidences of insecurity. We should be looking for solutions and those in authority should reward such intellectual efforts by adopting them. It should be clear to the discerning that terrorism, Fulani/indigene clashes, ethnic and religious strife and corruption are not really the problem of Nigeria. They are merely the symptoms of our problems. The main problem Nigeria has is that we have moved from a nation of about 50 million people in 1960 when we got independence from Britain, to a nation of close to 200 million people today.

While our population has quadrupled, opportunities have not quadrupled and in some cases they have reduced rather than increased. So the problem is that we have more people competing for fewer resources and when you have this scenario, civil strife is inevitable.

Factor in the dwindling revenue from oil, which is what fuelled our unprecedented population growth, and the situation is even more dire. The job of a leader in this type of situation is not to point a finger and say you are to blame and you are not to blame. No!

The job of a leader is to surround himself with people who know the root cause of problems and can come up with creative solutions to them because as Albert Einstein said: "No problem can be solved from the same level of consciousness that created it". If we have a roadmap for the future where cattle can be ranched in Nigeria by the Fulani and any other group that want to go into this form of business, Nigeria can become an exporter of beef thus turning a problem (Fulani/Indigene clash) into an opportunity. Some might read this and think this is far fetched, but they would be wrong.

About 10 years ago, a certain Fulani man named Abubakar Bukola Saraki introduced modern cattle ranching to Shonga in Kwara State when he, as Governor of Kwara State, invited the White Zimbabwean farmers that had lost their lands in Robert Mugabe's land redistribution programme to Nigeria. Saraki's government assisted the White Zimbabweans with financing, land and other necessary resources needed to resettle them in Nigeria. These farmers have successfully and profitably ranched cattle at Shonga and are contributing significantly to the economy of Kwara State and Nigeria without clashing with local farmers and other indigenes.

As a matter of fact, rather than clashes with the indigenes, they are employing the local farmers and indigenes and Shonga has become an epitome of peaceful coexistence in Nigeria. If one Fulani man in the person of Saraki can do this, then other Fulani can do it as well. There is money in cattle ranching. Make no mistake about it.

Take Argentina for example, 3 per cent of all exports out of Argentina is beef which provides an annual revenue of $5 billion to the Argentine government. Argentina provides 7.4 per cent of the world's beef exports and this is a market that has not been exhausted. There is room for growth in the global market for beef exports and Nigeria can key in to this by harnessing the resources of the Fulani through modern cattle ranches that will provide the domestic market with inexpensive beef and improve Nigeria's balance of trade position by exporting beef and cattle to other nations.

This will provide revenue for the government and jobs for the people.

This is Ben Murray Bruce and I just want to make common sense!
Published: 3rd August, 2015.

CHAPTER 10
TAME FUEL SUBSIDY OR
IT WILL TAME NIGERIA

If the whole idea of fuel subsidy is to pass on benefits to the poor, then we must all agree that it is not working. The benefits are going to importers of fuel, oil majors and upper and middle class Nigerians who can afford to live in the most urbanised areas of Nigeria which are the only places where fuel is still sold at the official rate.

Our people in the North-east and the Niger Delta have been buying petrol at black market prices for decades. Of what use is fuel subsidy to them? Is this not part of the reason why they sometimes feel alienated from Nigeria?

In the most recent data released by the International Monetary Fund (IMF), the Democratic Republic of Congo is rated the poorest nation in the world with a per capita income of less than $400. But the truth is that if you isolate the North-east of Nigeria from the rest of Nigeria and you compare their per capita income to that of the Congo DRC, it will be clear that the North-east of Nigeria is the poorest part of planet earth.

Yet, this poorest part of Nigeria is not really benefitting from what is meant to benefit them. And they are not alone. In the Niger Delta where I am from, particularly in Bayelsa which is my state, I have never bought fuel at the official rate. Fuel in the North-east and the Niger Delta goes for N300 per litre while fuel in Ikoyi in Lagos sells for N87!

Now tell me, who are we subsidising? The rich or the poor? You campaign in poetry but govern in prose. The time for poetry is gone. Now is a time for prose and the federal government must be creative enough to come up with ideas for passing on the benefits that the fuel subsidy is supposed to pass on to the poor but is not.

The federal government must also search out ideas on how Nigeria can generate more non oil income. As a patriotic duty, I will offer a few ideas on how

I think Nigeria can make the best use of her resources instead of spending it on an inefficient and corrupt subsidy that does not get to its intended recipients. In my opinion, the federal government should stop subsidising fuel and instead subsidise public transportation.

Now, how would this work?

The federal government must gather all the providers of mass transport, be it the National Union of Road Transport Workers (NURTW) or any of its affiliates and register all of them in a central database. Next, the federal government must find out what the unit cost of transporting an individual passenger costs.

Then the federal government should sign an agreement that it would pay the increased cost of a unit of transport that would ensue when fuel subsidy is abolished and the oil market is deregulated.

To ensure fidelity and prevent fraud, each individual provider (be it a bus, a boat or any other transport type that uses premium motor spirit) must covenant to buy their fuel exclusively from Nigerian National Petroleum Corporation (NNPC) petrol stations (or a petrol station chain that can be monitored by the federal government) and also agree to have a fuel monitor installed into their vehicles.

The monitor will report the amount of petrol consumed by each unit of transportation and at the end of the month, the federal government, through the Petroleum Products Pricing Regulatory Agency (PPPRA) would reimburse the provider the excess money paid for fuel as a result of the deregulation and the lifting of the subsidy on premium motor spirit.

In this manner, the federal government will be able to deregulate the downstream sector of the oil and gas industry while at the same time providing relief for the poorest Nigerians from the effect of an increase in the price of fuel.

Moreover, the federal government can spend a fraction of the trillions of naira we are currently spending on fuel subsidy annually on social services that will have a direct impact on the well being of the poorest of the poor and boost out Human Development Index.

For instance, Nigeria can reduce infant and maternal mortality rates, by initiating a Women, Infants and Children (WIC) Intervention Programme in all the states of the federation.

The programme could be an initiative of the federal government through the Ministry of Health and would involve giving free pre and ante natal supplements to pregnant and nursing mothers and one infant per family up to the age of five. In addition to receiving these vitamin supplements, each recipient should be given a crate of eggs each week and at least one tin of evaporated milk per day on a weekly, biweekly or monthly basis.

Doing so would have a direct impact on the health of the most vulnerable subsection of our population, women, infants and children up to the age of five. Desperate times call for desperate remedies and in case we have not noticed, these are desperate times. Oil is fast losing its value. A world without oil is a reality. Nigeria must start thinking of other ways of growing her economy that does not depend on oil.

If we really want to build our economy, we may want to take a cue from what India and China did. The economies of both countries have been built up to be amongst the world's leading economies largely through the efforts of their Diaspora citizens who returned home after having established themselves in Europe and the Americas.

In the 80s, Nigeria suffered from a massive brain drain when our most educated intellectuals left the country for greener pastures after conditions in the nation's Ivory Towers proved too oppressive for them. We can use a fraction of what we are spending on the fuel subsidy to facilitate a brain gain.

All over the world, Nigerians in the Diaspora are having children who are enrolled in some of the best schools world wide. Many of these universities have internship programmes that allow students intern anywhere in the world. I propose that the federal government should seize the initiative and initiate a bring back the brain scheme whereby the Federal Government of Nigeria through her MDAs (perhaps the Ministry of Education, the National Universities Commission, NUC, or the Industrial Training Fund, ITF) actively solicits for children of Nigerians in the Diaspora to return to Nigeria to do their internship.

This initiative may be promoted by roadshows in the major cities of the world, via Nigerian tribal or ethnic organisations in the Diaspora. Our embassies could be mandated to dedicate some staff to tour universities in their host countries in order to sell this idea to the students directly. The federal government may encourage those wishing to participate by offering to pay their return tickets and instruct that all MDAs that participate in the scheme should pay the accommodation costs of these students during their internship. The expected result of this scheme is a net inflow of skilled labour into Nigeria to drive our developmental effort.

Many of these highly educated and skilled expatriate children will opt to remain behind and establish businesses or use their education and experience abroad to improve businesses already in existence. This is what happened in the Asian Tigers. We should not re-invent the wheel. Let us simply do in Nigeria what others have done with great success.

Also, the federal government has to find a way to encourage Nigerians to return to agriculture either as a business or by way of subsistence farming as a way of reducing our dependence on imported food on which we spend over a trillion naira annually.

The other day, I was shocked by the data from the Central Bank of Nigeria (CBN) stating that we spend N813 billion annually on staples like sugar, wheat and other food items that we have the capacity of producing ourselves in Nigeria. N813 billion importing sugar and wheat? Really? Nigerians will not die if we do not import sugar and fish. So why must we import them? We must learn to drink plain tea until we can make our own sugar.

And then it turns out that we spent another N100 billion annually importing toothpicks and furniture? Really? We need foreigners to help us pick our teeth? According to the report, the amount spent on importing rice, sugar, wheat, fish, furniture, milk and textiles in 2013 is equal to one-fifth of the country's total budget of about N4 trillion. With the deal Iran is entering into with America, the oil price is likely to reduce again. Can Nigeria continue spending N1 trillion on food imports?

What a waste. The federal government must cut this waste. We cannot afford to be gradual with this. We will not die if we do not eat sugar, wheat and these other items. Necessity is the mother of invention. If we must have them then we should produce them! This is by no means the limit of the ideas that can help grow Nigeria's economy and help us apply our finances to areas of growth rather than areas of waste, but it is a beginning.

In the 1980s, the Directorate of Mass Mobilisation for Self Reliance, Social Justice, and Economic Recovery (MAMSER) had a TV advertisement that went thus 'oil go finish one day o, no let water pass garri ooo!' That day has come. Has water passed garri? That is the million dollar question no one has an answer to. Nigeria has a lot of work to do. Two thousand years ago Rome knew how many people it had. Mary and Joseph were counted in Bethlehem. In 2015, does Nigeria know how many people she has? If we do not know how many people we have, how can we make effective planning decisions on which to base our economic strategies on?

This is a question for another day.

I just want to make common sense!
Published: 24th July, 2015.

Chapter 11
We Need More Brain Infrastructure!

All the conspiracy theories about the Boko Haram uprising collapse when you consider the data painstakingly acquired by the Africa Health, Human & Social Development Information Service (Afri-Dev).

I was just going through the data the other day and my thinking was that our chickens are coming home to roost.

Nigeria has neglected education for so long and the grim statistics leave us no hiding place.

According to the data 52.4% of males in the Northeastern region of Nigeria have no formal Western education. This represents the highest level of illiteracy among men in the federation.

It is therefore not surprising that the Northeast is also the most insecure part of Nigeria.

46.9 % of the adult male population of the Northwestern region have no formal Western education. Again, the pattern is consistent as the Northwest is the second most insecure region of Nigeria.

But it is not until you begin to look at the trend on a state by state basis that you see even more clearly the connection between illiteracy and insecurity.

Yobe and Borno have the highest illiteracy levels in the country and the two states are precisely the states at the epicenter of insecurity in Nigeria.

A whopping 83.3% of boys over 6 and adult men in Yobe state have no formal Western education. The figure for Borno which is number two on the list is 63.6%.

The data from Afri-Dev is proof positive that the only sustainable way to fight insecurity in Nigeria is through education not guns and bombs.

Nowhere has this been more demonstrated than in Anambra state.

Before the election of Peter Obi as governor of Anambra state, the state was notorious as the kidnap capital of Nigeria. It also featured prominently when other violent crimes were mentioned. But most telling was the fact that the state was considered backward in boy child education.

Now let us pause for a while and note that most violent crimes are committed by males.

Now by 2013, according to the official results released by the West African Senior School Certificate Examination (WASSCE), Anambra state had the highest percentage of students who passed the examinations with a pas rate of 67.85%. This from a state that used to be at the bottom!

If you thought that was a fluke one time occurrence, then consider that the state bettered that performance in 2014, again emerging the number one state with a pass mark of 65.92%.

So, how did Peter Obi achieve the feat of turning an educationally backward state like Anambra to the front runner amongst the most educated states?

Careful study of the budgetary allocation of the Peter Obi administration will reveal the answer.

During his years as governor, Obi ensured that education had the highest sectoral allocation. He also ensured that capital allocation consistently dwarfed recurrent expenditure which meant he spent more money building schools, roads and hospitals than he did paying salaries.

For instance, in his last year as governor, Anambra's budget was 140 billion Naira. 73% of that budget (100.29 billion Naira) was earmarked for capital expenditure, while only 27% (39.71 billion Naira) was earmarked for recurrent expenditure.

That year, as in subsequent years, Obi allocated the highest sectoral allocation to education (7.172 billion Naira).

The secret to Obi's success in education is increased spending on Capital projects and reduced spending on recurrent expenditure as well as giving education the highest sectoral allocation.

It is worthy of note that those states that are poorer than Anambra and which actually suffer from high levels of insecurity budgeted more than the 7.172 billion Naira that Anambra budgeted on education for security!

For instance, in 2014, Ambassador Baba Jidda, the then Secretary to the Borno State Government revealed that Borno state had spent over 10 billion Naira on security!

The facts are clear that when spending on education increases, insecurity will reduce within a year or two. However, when spending on security increases, there is no data that shows that insecurity also reduces.

The facts are also clear that when education levels increase, crime and insecurity reduce. When education levels drop, crime and insecurity increase.

Another state which proves this is Kano. Kudos goes to the people of Kano and to their immediate past Governor, Rabiu Musa Kwankwaso.

What Kano achieved under Kwankwaso could qualify as a modern day miracle.

The state used to be one of the most educationally backward states in the country which in itself was a big cause for concern bearing in mind that Kano has the highest population of any state in Nigeria.

Faced with the startling reality before him, then governor Kwankwaso, through a number of agencies most notable of which is the Kano State Agency for Mass Education, set about to increase literacy levels to an ambitious 90%.

Kwankwaso instituted the policy of free education for all Kano indigenes up to tertiary levels and began to give education the highest sectoral allocation.

For instance, in 2014, he budgeted 21 billion Naira for education. The Kano state government also set up 8,074 adult literacy classes in 484 electoral wards in the 44 local government councils of the state. They made it easy for people to access education.

The end result of this proactive leadership is that literacy rates in Kano state have increased from 48.9 in 2010 (according to the United Nations Education, Scientific and Cultural Organization, UNESCO) to over 60% in 2015.

Now let us again pause and consider that although Boko Haram has been trying to make inroads into Kano state, they have never been able to gain a foot hold. This is pleasantly surprising when you consider that in previous decades, similar sects like Maitatsine had used Kano state as a launch pad for their nefarious activities.

What has changed between December 1980, when thousands were killed in Kano following an uprising by the Maitatsine sect and today? The change is that today, education levels in Kano are dramatically higher than they were in December 1980, thus, the conditions are not ripe for terrorism to flourish there.

What has happened in Kano and Anambra state proves while clearly that where there is the political will to improve education, education does improve.

Nigeria is currently spending 72% of our income paying salaries and other recurrent expenditure with little or nothing left for capital expenditure.

We are even at the point where we have to borrow to pay salaries because we prefer to use our wealth to fund an unsustainable fuel subsidy.

We keep on giving our people this fuel subsidy fish instead of teaching them how to fish through education.

If at all we must subsidize anything, shouldn't it be education?

The people of the Northeast have been buying petrol at black market prices for decades. Of what use is fuel subsidy to them!

Right now they are not benefitting from fuel subsidy or education subsidy and the result is that they have become vulnerable to the most violent form of terrorism on planet earth and they are not alone. That terrorism is spreading fast and we cannot recruit soldiers fast enough to combat it.

When a nation wastes the minds of her youth by not providing them access to education, those youths will waste that nation.

If a nation does not invest her wealth educating her youth, that nation will invest that same wealth fighting insecurity amongst those same youth.

And when I say a nation, I do not just mean the nation state called Nigeria. I refer to all of us who have capacity including individuals and corporate bodies.

Right there in Borno, where poverty and illiteracy in Western education is most abysmal, are some of the most expensive houses and villas in Nigeria. Maiduguri probably has more oil multi millionaires per square mile than any other state capital with the possible exception of Lagos state.

What have these individuals done in their personal capacity to develop the educational capacity of children of the peasants around them?

I am not from the East, but I admire the custom of our brothers from that part of the country to take community development as a core duty of any individual that has the means.

They do not wait for government to build schools or roads or hospitals or even airports. Men of means within their community pool resources and build these facilities and in that way the community is made more prosperous. And the more prosperous the community is, the more secure the men of means within that community are.

I urge other communities across Nigeria to learn from this community spirit displayed by the South-easterners.

Let me give a modern day parable of how care for society benefits the person who cares.

A rich man was traveling in a convoy to his village. He had police escorts and they made his journey easier.

About an hour to his destination, he met some traffic and his police escorts maneuvered his convoy through the traffic.

He noticed that the traffic was caused by an accident involving two cars which blocked the road. He could have asked his police escorts to intervene, but he could not be bothered, after all they were ordinary people.

Soon, this rich man got to his village and entered his mansion and began to make himself feel at home. And then suddenly, he had a heart attack.

His wife quickly called a doctor to rush down to the village to attend to him. And then the family waited and waited and waited.

Eventually the man died. Ten minutes after he died, his doctor arrived. Enraged, the man's family accosted him and asked why he had only just arrived.

'Do you realize you could have saved my husband's life if you had arrived just ten minutes earlier' the man's wife screamed.

The flustered doctor apologized and said 'I would have arrived more than an hour ago but for some traffic I met on the way. The people told me that some police passed by and did not help them. If only the police had helped them I would have been here earlier'.

You see, by not helping less privileged people in need, the rich man ended up escalating an incident that led to his own death.

Almost 100% of Nigeria's elite achieved the success they have today because leaders like Chief Obafemi Awolowo, Sir Ahmadu Bello and Nnamdi Azikiwe ensured that they benefited from free education. Yet, after climbing up the education ladder, we have removed the ladder that got us there instead of perpetuating it!

I call on our elite to show more concern to their places of origin. Help to educate the less privileged in your village or community.

If you can build a school, then build one beside your mansion. Do not just wait until Ramadan or Christmas to give out food to the poor. Give them education and they will learn how to feed themselves.

If you cannot build schools, then buy books for the children of the less privileged. If you cannot buy books, why not volunteer to teach in the local primary school in your village whenever you are home? You will 'oppress' the people more when you impart knowledge into their kids than you would with your latest SUV!

Yes, stomach infrastructure is necessary, but even more necessary is brain infrastructure. Why? Because education is key. A hungry man is hungry for one day but an uneducated man is hungry forever.

I just want to make common sense!
Published: 14th July, 2015.

CHAPTER 12
A THIRD ALTERNATIVE TO PDP AND APC

Months after the 2015 elections ended, Nigerian youths are still hung up on those elections. Nowhere is this more obvious than on social media which our youths have turned to a battle ground divided into pro People Democratic Party (PDP) and pro All Progressives Congress (APC) youths. So ingrained is this animosity that each group targets elected officials and party chieftains of the opposing parties and go after them just on the basis of their party affiliation. Things reached a comical stage when a youth attacked me for a tweet on Twitter and hours later was praising a popular youth for his tweet. Unbeknownst to him was the fact that the youth had merely tweeted my exact words but had not credited me with the quote!

These shenanigans makes me concerned for our youth. Where they should be getting closer and breaking down barriers, they are holding a candle for politicians who in reality are not as divided as they lead these youths to believe.

For instance, Senator Bukola Saraki is the Senate President and Chairman of the National Assembly today. He could not have been elevated to that exalted seat were it not for the votes of senators of the PDP. What does that teach us? It teaches us that all politicians are divided by a common interest which united them when the conditions are right and temporarily divides them when they are wrong.

I advise youths not to look at Nigeria from a pro PDP or APC perspective. They should see the country from a pro youth outlook. Their future is greater than a party. Nigerian youths should not believe and act as if the only options available to them are either the PDP or the APC. There is a third alternative.

This third alternative is patriotism.

I am reminded of the wise words of Mark Twain who defined patriotism as "loyalty to the country always. Loyalty to the government when it deserves it". Our youths have to imbibe this wisdom from Mark Twain and refrain from saying and tweeting nasty stuff about each other and their religions, regions, tribes and ethnicities.

Those who engage in this do not understand that foreigners follow Twitter trends and when our youths are disrespecting each other's ethnicities and religions, they must realise that foreigners do not see us as Yoruba, Hausa and Igbo. They just see us as Nigerians. I therefore advise our youths and indeed all Nigerians to speak of Nigeria in a way that shows the world that we value her. If we put a small price on Nigeria, we should be rest assured that the world will not raise that price.

We should not come on social media to abuse one another on partisan grounds. That to me is an abuse of the platform.

I am sure Jack Dorsey, Noah Glass, Biz Stone and Evan Williams, who founded Twitter, did not found it as a platform where we come to outdo each other in raining insults on those on the opposite political divide from us. Speaking for myself, I am on Twitter to release my ideas for scrutiny and receive ideas of other Twitter users for contemplation, because none of us is as smart as all of us.

Our youths need to understand that we are living in an idea age not an insult age. It takes interdependence and interconnection to create the atmosphere that inspires brilliant ideas. Our youths are short circuiting this interconnection when they alienate each other.

And I am aghast as to what to say to those elders who come on Twitter and fan the embers of division amongst our youths by retweeting them when they retweet insults and destructive criticism against their political opponents. Even worse is when they praise them by calling them intelligent for engaging in this behaviour.

We really need to watch it. Nigerian youths are beginning to define intelligence as the ability to come up with the most sophisticated insult and criticism. We urgently need to redefine intelligence in Nigeria. Mudslinging, cynicism and criticism are not acts of intelligence. Ideas and creativity are. If you are truly intelligent, you won't be on Twitter lobbing insults on political opponents. Instead you will be tweeting ideas that inspire solutions to Nigeria's challenges!

I want to urge these elders, who I have come to be aware are called Twitter overlords, to remember that true elders plant trees of peace even though they know they may never benefit from the shades of those trees.

President Barack Obama, Senator Hillary Clinton and former President Bill Clinton are some of the most criticised political figures in the world, but they do not use social media to react to the criticism they receive. Instead, conscious of the fact that their role is to set good moral standards for the youths, they constantly tweet uplifting and inspiring tweets which have the capacity to unite people. That is what we should do as elders in Nigeria. If we do not do this, we should consider that a time may come when those attack dogs have savaged all our enemies, and having nothing else to savage they may turn on us.

This is Ben Murray Bruce and I just want to make common sense.
Published: 6th July, 2015.

Chapter 13
Presidential Fleet: Cutting Nigeria's Coat According to Her Cloth

On the 10th of May 2015, I tweeted the following "Left to me, we must sell the Presidential fleet. Public servants, including the President must only use made in Nigeria Peugeot as official car!". I really believe what I tweeted and was overjoyed when the media reported that President Muhammadu Buhari had ordered the sale of nine presidential jets. My joy was however cut short when the Presidency denied those reports and said the president had not taken such a decision. Nigeria may perhaps be the only country in the world without a national air carrier whose presidential fleet is larger than many airlines.

This was wasteful in the years of our oil boom, but in this current dispensation of reduced income from oil, it actually makes no sense to maintain the presidential air fleet. Recently, I tweeted that we should start compulsorily teaching our youths entrepreneurial skills from primary school through university and when they graduate they should spend their National Youth Service Corps (NYSC) years in an entrepreneurial finishing programme and upon satisfactorily completing of the programme each corps member should receive N5,000 in the form of a bank guarantee to pay for setting up a Small and Medium Scale Enterprise (SME).

A youth who liked the idea tweeted back at me and asked me how Nigeria could pay for this.

Well, Nigeria presently spends on average N5 billion (5.3 billion in the 2015 budget) to maintain the Presidential Air Fleet (PAF). This is not the value of the fleet. It is just the amount used to maintain the 11 planes in the fleet. This amount can be used to provide business start-up grants of over five N500,000 to 10,000 NYSC members. So, in answer to Okikiola Raymond @DonOkizle, who is the youth who asked me that question, Nigeria can pay for it with the money we are currently using to maintain our PAF and other wasteful expenditures.

We need a common sense revolution and though I know it is not practical, I almost wish President Buhari would appoint a minister for common sense!

Does it make sense that our presidential fleet is larger than that of the Queen of England?

Does it make sense that our president flies to a G-7 meeting to ask for financial and technical assistance in a presidential jet that is either as expensive or more expensive than the planes that conveyed some of the G-7 leaders to Germany? Nigeria has failed woefully to wean itself from oil and we really should begin taking drastic measures to wean ourselves otherwise we will suck mother Nigeria dry and then what! I always fly Arik to any destination I am headed. The only exception is where Arik does not fly that route.

Many people will be surprised to note that Aliko Dangote, the richest black man on planet earth, flies Arik just as I do. Yes, Arik has challenges, but those challenges are not insurmountable and they will be better able to surmount them if you and I patronise Arik. I do not have a single share in Arik, but I have stakeholder interests in Nigeria and Arik flies the Nigerian flag. When our big boys buy a British Airways ticket, they are helping to service the British economy and pay for salaries there. That money leaves Nigeria and circulates in England where it helps shore up the value of the British Pound Sterling.

Let me tell you of an experience I had. I once flew from Paris to Abuja (Arik doesn't fly that route) on an Air France flight. An air hostess approached me and asked me to join their Frequent Flyer programme where upon I asked her if it was similar to British Airways' programme. I was taken aback when she began appealing to me not to fly BA but stick to Air France. She brought her colleagues and they gave me gifts on board and ensured me they would look after me if I continued to fly Air France. This is the behaviour of people who love their country. They believe in her and sell her and promote her to others even where it does not bring any specific pecuniary interest to them.

I appeal to President Buhari to sell off our presidential jet and in addition to that he should consider issuing an Executive Order mandating all government officials to fly Nigerian airlines except in those cases where a Nigerian airline does not fly to the destination in which they are headed. President Buhari should take a cue from President Joyce Banda of Malawi who not only sold off that country's presidential jet, but also sold off 60 Mercedes Benz limousines attached to her Presidency. So impressed was he by President Banda's move that Andrew Mitchell, the UK International Development Secretary, immediately handed over 32 million pounds of British Aid to her government.

Malawi had only one presidential jet and 60 Mercedes Benz limousines. Nigeria currently has at least 11 presidential jets and hundreds of Mercedes Benz cars in her inventory. These are depreciating assets that add value to only a few people at the top. If we do the commonsensical thing and sell off these luxury items and apply the savings towards developing the entrepreneurial skills of our youths, we will spark off a revolution that will see our youths re-channelling their minds and energies away from Boko Haram terrorism, kidnapping, pipeline vandalism, Internet fraud into positive endeavours like enterprise and innovation.

Asked about her decision to sell off her presidential jet, Mrs Banda said "I can as well use private airlines. I am already used to hitchhiking". That is a leader! She cuts her coat according to her nation's cloth not according to its size. This is the best advice for Nigeria at this point in time. We can take it or we can continue to spend billions maintaining our Presidential Air Fleet!

Published: 22nd June, 2015.

CHAPTER 14
EMPOWERING OUR YOUTHS THROUGH SPORTS AND ENTERTAINMENT

In a country of 175 million people where over 100 million people are youths, the most important ministry is not the ministry of finance or the ministry of petroleum. It is the ministry of youths!

Nigeria has spent decades living off the minerals under her ground, especially oil, and we as a nation have forgotten that the most valuable resource we have are our people and especially our youth.

Nigeria is still operating under a colonial era mentality whereby minerals, raw materials and cash crops are regarded as assets and people are regarded as liabilities.

This is why Nigerian leaders misunderstand the term employment. Employment refers to being occupied. It involves utilizing ones mental and physical energies in a rewarding manner.

In practical terms, it is impossible to immediately provide paid employment for all our youths in the short term.

There is a law of process involved in achieving that aim.

However, we can and we should provide our youths other activities through which they can positively employ their mental and physical energies.

Sports is one of those activities. We have stadia that lie fallow all over Nigeria. Until recently, the national stadium in Abuja was overgrown with weeds as are other stadia.

The ministry of youths should collaborate with the ministry of sports to throw them open and encourage youths to utilize the facilities.

Our stadia and sports facilities should not only be used to host the very occasional football games. They should be used to positively employ the minds and bodies of our youth in positive activities.

With only a small amount of money we can keep these facilities running and available to our youth. The devil finds work for idle hands. If we keep

Our youths positively employed, they will not be armed robbers, Boko Haram terrorist or area boys.

And Nigeria as a country has been making efforts to make one people out of many people. Unity has been a recurring challenge as many Nigerians cling to primordial and regional sentiments over national sentiments.

What can unite a country better than sports? Who can unite a country better than youths?

Nigeria is at its most united state when we are playing a game of soccer against another country or competing in an athletic meet with other nations.

Since we know that, let us use sports and games to both unite the nation and redirect the energy of our youth towards something positive.

Nigeria needs to prioritize the ministry of youths. Quality brains should be appointed and employed as minister, Permanent Secretary and directors. These should be people with ideas, who know the value of recreation as a means of engendering productivity in our young people.

President Muhammadu Buhari has repeatedly said he wants to create employment for our youth.

We can create employment through sports.

The ministry of sports must remake itself from being a ministry of football to a ministry that impacts Nigeria.

As a former Director General of the Nigerian Television Authority, I know that sophisticated cameras, that can shoot underwater and in high altitudes, were bought for the 2003 All Africa Games in Abuja. There were others that were also bought for the 1999 FIFA World Youth Championship (U-20 World Cup) which held in Nigeria.

NTA has cameras and equipment that can be used to cover every Olympic sport. NTA also has outside broadcasting vans.

We do not have to limit ourselves to going to the Olympics and the All Africa Games every four years.

We can institute a national sporting event to occupy our youths and also identify talents. In the past we used to have Mobil Track and Field events every year, but ever since ExxonMobil pulled out in 2011, we have not been able to replicate a national track and field event of such a magnitude.

The ministry of sports has all that is required to revive that event even without private sponsorship. As a matter of fact, if you revive it, the private sponsors will come.

Nigeria can project her greatness via sport, but we are short changing ourselves if we do not invest in sports as a way to channel the creative energies of our youths into positive ventures.

As a child, I idolized Dick Tiger, the first African to win an international boxing title when won the world middleweight boxing championship in 1962.

Dick Tiger was discovered when a British prize fighter came to Nigeria and offered anyone who could knock him out the sum of three guineas. Of course an unknown young man named Richard Ihetu (Dick Tiger's real name) knocked him out and the rest is history.

If that Briton did not come to Nigeria, Richard Ihetu would never have become Dick Tiger.

I cannot help but wonder how many Dick Tigers we are missing out on every year.

And even in football, the one sport that we have concentrated on, we are not maximizing the opportunities that professional football brings to a country.

In England in 2013, 32% of the population were actively engaged in one way or the other with the English Premiership League. The League itself made a revenue of over £3 Billion in 2013 (that is money the EPL made for itself alone). In 2012, 900,000 foreign fans came to England to attend Barclays Premier League matches and spent £706 Million. 1.5 Billion people watch the English Premiership League worldwide. They buy merchandise from Britain, keeping the British people employed and prosperous. Britain made over £2 Billion in the 2013 by selling overseas broadcasting rights to the EPL.

As an example of how the EPL contributes to job growth, in 2011, when

Swansea City was promoted to the EPL, that promotion led to 295 new full time jobs being created in the small town of Swansea, and the promotion attracted tourists who spent £8.13 million in Swansea in that season.

In short, sports and especially football, can generate jobs and boost our Gross Domestic Product if developed.

What is wrong if the President personally goes to watch matches in the Nigeria Premier League? What is wrong if he directs his ministers to do likewise?

Imagine the impact on the popularity and acceptability of the Nigeria Premier League if the public sees the President and top Nigerians at their matches rather than at British Matches? British Prime Minister, David Cameron does it, German Chsncellor, Angela Merkel, does it. Why can't our leaders do it?

It will boost the popularity of the league which will attract sponsors which will attract big broadcasters which will make it international which will attract foreign investments which will create JOBS!

Our youths need jobs and because we are not creating enough job opportunities for them, they are terrorizing us all over the country.

We have to be creative with ideas to lift Nigeria out of the doldrums and launch her into orbit as one of the world's economic power houses.

Even if we start out now with a plan to compete with the West and the Asian Tigers in the area of technology and manufacturing, it will take us at least one generation to make any meaningful impact, if at all.

But we have areas of comparative advantage as a nation and if we focus on those areas, we can reach and surpass what has been done in the West and Asia.

One of the areas where we have a comparative advantage is in the motion picture industry.

Nollywood is now the third largest movie industry in the world. The industry has been driven by the raw talent of the Nigerian youth and the grit of largely Idumota based marketers and their international chain.

Nollywood is a youth driven industry. When you support Nollywood, you are giving Nigerian youths an escape that gives them hope and helps them cope with the duality challenges of being a youth in a nation like Nigeria.

Government may think that Nollywood is just entertainment, but they will be very wrong if we think that. No one buys into your industrial and manufacturing complex except they first buy your culture.

Western governments understand this which is why President Obama got personally involved when North Korea threatened Sony Pictures over the movie 'The Interview'.

Culture projection is the first vital step in winning the hearts and minds of a people. It has been done since time immemorial.

It is the reason the British always sent in their missionaries that propagated their particular Christian denomination in the areas they wanted to colonize. After selling their culture, they then sent in their merchants.

It is the reason Nigerian youths are so crazy about European Premiership Football. We first of all fall in love with European Football and next we start going to Europe on holiday to spend our hard earned cash.

Michael Jackson was the first black artist to be played on MTV and when White America fell in love with him, they bought into Black culture and because they bought into Black culture, Black cultural icons like Jayz, Dr. Dre and P Diddy took it to the next level and became business mogul selling products of black origin to first White America, then the rest of the world. Now, Apple has made Dr. Dre a billionaire by buying 'Beats by Dr. Dre' for $3 billion.

What the Buhari administration ought to do, if it is truly interested in creating jobs, is to continue the unprecedented support that industry enjoyed during the Jonathan years.

No other administration in Nigeria's history supported Nollywood as much as the Jonathan administration. He gave them a grant of 3 Billion Naira to develop capacity and he encouraged them with his presence at their industry wide events.

This helped Nollywood shoot quality movies that can be entered in for international film competitions like the Academy Awards, the Cannes Film Festival and the Montreal Film Festival.

The more visibility Nolywood gets, the more the image of the average Nigerian is rehabilitated. The more the image of Nigeria is rehabilitated, the more the world buys into Nigerian brands like Glo, UBA, Dangote Cement etc.

Going forward, whoever President Buhari appoints as minister of culture has to work with the President's protocol people to include Nollywood icons in his entourage when he travels abroad. The minister of Sports has to do the same with sports stars and our international athletes. This will help transfer some of the goodwill and credibility these icons have amassed on both the President and the country.

We just had President Buhari's inauguration and look who the US sent-John Kerry (the US Secretary of State) and Akeem Olajuwon!

The US was not being sentimental when they chose Akeem. No! He is a US citizen and a well loved sports icon. They know that if he is seen in their official delegation, those who see him will associate the warmth and goodwill they feel for him with America.

If those people are government officials, which they are likely to be, then they become more likely to tilt Nigerian foreign policy towards America.

If they are business leaders, they are more likely to award contracts to American companies and buy American products.

If they are ordinary Nigerians, they are more likely to want to spend their holidays and their hard earned money in America and on American products.

Do we see the multiplier effect?

And finally, together with the minister of information, the minister of culture should be a custodian of our national culture and historical records.

We do not document our leaders and their highs and lows and their successes and failures and as George Santayana said "those who cannot remember the past are condemned to repeat it"!

That is why we keep repeating the sake mistakes over and over again as a nation.

Nigerians may be surprised to note that if you want to get accurate records of the Nigerian Civil War, of Supreme Military Council activities of leaders that were deposed (eg Buhari's first regime), of defining moments of Nigeria's history, you have to go to either the British Broadcasting Corporation, BBC or the British ITV.

What does that say of us as a nation and as a people?

Published: 8th June, 2015.

Chapter 15
Buhari and Mutually Assured Restoration!

In the run up to his inauguration, President-elect, Muhammadu Buhari, has been telling the nation of his plans and policy direction and one of those policies is his stated intention to resume the search for oil in Northern Nigeria and specifically in the Lake Chad region of Borno State. Ironically, Borno is one of the states ravaged by the scourge of terrorism which has set that state and the entire Northeast region back in almost every index of human development.

If oil is found in the Lake Chad region, it will go a long way in reviving the economy of the Northeast. However, Buhari's plan has met with some criticism especially in the South were a number of pundits and analysts see the plan as an expensive wild goose chase that would not yield anything.

I believe we are being short sighted when we criticize such a plan. Nigeria needs multiple streams of income now more than ever. And if Niger and Chad have struck oil in commercial quantities, it stands to reason that the chances of oil being found in Northern Nigeria and especially the Lake Chad region are higher than we had previously thought when we abandoned the search for oil in that region over a decade ago.

Any student of economics will tell you that Nigeria will be more balanced if we can find commercial oil deposits up North.

It is just natural. Nature abhors unipolarity and favours bipolarity. That is why things come with a balance. Night and day, hot and cold, up and down, bitter and sweet, fast and slow are examples.

The world was a much safer place because of the Mutually Assured Destruction (MAD) doctrine which saw the then Union of Soviet Socialist Republics (USSR) now Russia having an almost equal ability with the United States to assure each other's destruction which meant that they would never go to war directly against each other. They balanced each other out.

However, there was a brief period when only the United States had nuclear weapons and that was the only period in human history when nuclear weapons were used.

Do you see how it works? When there was no balance, there was nothing to stop the US from using atomic weapons. But when nature or the divine corrected that imbalance with the rise of the Soviet bloc there was a check on West and vice versa.

Balance is a good thing.

We can relate this to Nigeria. As long as the overwhelming majority of Nigeria's revenue comes from oil which is located almost exclusively in the Niger Delta and states contiguous to the region, Nigeria will be vulnerable to shocks of a unipolar economy.

Anything that affects the oil bearing region will continue to threaten the rest of the nation and once the actors in that play have tasted this power and no what it is to take action that affects global oil prices, it is going to be hard to persuade them not to use such influence when they feel wronged.

It is just like the saying that when all you have is a hammer, everything looks like a nail.

But if we are able to find oil in commercial quantities in the North as Buhari hopes, then Nigeria would have a balance of scenarios such that if there are tantrums being thrown in one of the theaters, we could afford to damn those actors and push ahead in the other theater until things return to normal.

Such a situation, in my opinion, will ensure that neither side has any incentive to initiate a crisis.

It is like a plane. The reason why planes have two engines is not because an aircraft requires both engines to fly. No! A plane can fly and land at its destination with one engine.

The problem is that if that engine should fail in the air, the plane would crash, so it is safer to have two engines such that if one of them fails the other becomes the back up.

The reason our economy is looking like it will crash, with perhaps half of the states in Nigeria owing workers salary and refusing to take responsibility for it and instead blaming the Federal Government, is because we have only one stream of major income coming largely from one region.

In other words, we have only one engine! We seriously need another engine and if Buhari is the man to look for that second engine for Nigeria then he has my support and deserves the support of all Nigerians.

Because if he is successful (and the chances are good that he will) Nigeria will enjoy the opposite of what the USSR and The US had, a Mutually Assured Restoration.

It is not surprising that Buhari's plan to invest funds in the search for oil in the North is unpopular in the South.

Many Southerners erroneously think the North is dependent on the South. In actual fact, the reverse is the case!

The most basic human need after oxygen is food. If the North is dependent on the South for foreign exchange, then the South must know that she is dependent on the North for her food security.

Nations can survive without oil, but they cannot survive without food and many of our staple foods be it Rice, locally grown wheat, cows on the hoof, tomatoes, peppers onions etc, come from the North.

The point I am trying to make is that we need each other and we have to move from a philosophy of competition between North and South to one of cooperation.

And many of the stereotypes we hold of Northerners down south are not true at all.

Many Southerners see the North and Northerners as a backward Muslim people adverse to Western education who would rather not stay in Nigeria except that they cannot survive on their own without the South.

So when Southerners read that a community like Chibok, in the core North is overwhelmingly Christian, their stereotype is challenged.

When they become aware that the richest black man and African on the planet is from the core Northern state of Kano their stereotype is challenged.

When they realize that a very large proportion of the population of the North is educated, that stereotype becomes questionable.

And, yes, a very large proportion of the North is educated!

The issue is that because we see education as a Western phenomenon we fail to look at it holistically and historically, thereby believing that if you are not Western educated then you are not educated. But that is far from the truth!

Centuries before many in the South learnt to read and write in the English language, our Northern brothers and sisters have been writing in a quasi indigenous script called the Ajami script.

Hausa has been written in ajami, since the early 15th century. There are centuries old literary material and letters written in this script and you must have respect for people who developed intellectual learning methods long before Western civilization came to our shores.

Many of us read about Uthman Dan Fodio in history, but unfortunately, contemporary history has limited his role in Nigeria's evolution to that of a jihadist fighter. In actual fact, Uthman Dan Fodio was a scholar. Even that word 'Fodio' is Fufulde for scholar or learned one.

His own mother, Hauwa and his grand mother, Rukayya, were also 'fodios' and taught others. This is in the 17th century mind you.

The fact is that long before Western education arrived the shores of Southern Nigeria, Northern Nigeria had already experienced centuries of indigenous and Arabic education.

So let us begin to shatter our stereotypes of each other and accept each other based on the fact that if God did not desire it to be so, we would not be Nigerians.

Having found ourselves as Nigerians, let us make the best of it by using our energies to work together so we can make progress, rather than using if to fight each other in a Mutually Assured Destruction (MAD).

I am all for a Mutually Assured Restoration and I urge all Nigerians, both Northern and Southern, to understand our differences (because it is foolishness to think that we can forget them) and learn to coexist in peace and prosperity.

Published: 26th May, 2015.

Chapter 16
Death to Xenophobia and Tribalism!

To paraphrase George Bernard Shaw, Nigeria and South Africa are two countries separated by a common language and a common bond. There are too many shared interests between the two nations and as such both nations must work as partners rather than rivals.

The issue of the recent wave of xenophobia in South Africa is unfortunate, but we must not throw away the baby with the bath water. Just as terrorism occasioned by the Boko Haram sect should not define Nigeria, xenophobia should not define South Africa.

As a government and as a people, we must show South Africa, at the very minimum, the same level of tolerance their government and people showed to us when 84 of their citizens died at the synagogue building collapse in Nigeria.

Let us learn something positive about this issue. If it is wrong to hate people because they are foreigners in your country, it must equally be wrong to hate fellow citizens because they are from a different tribe or region or religion. Charity begins at home. African nations, including Nigeria, must address prejudices such as tribalism and religious intolerance at home because the best way to get others to love you is to first love yourself.

This has always been my desire for the Black Race. No one put it as good as the late Peter Tosh in his song 'African' when he sang "don't care where you come from As long as you're a black man, you're an African. No mind your nationality, you have got the identity of an African".

Peter Tosh was a prophet. As long as we are a part of the Black Race, we all have the identity of an African.

There is nothing to be ashamed of about being an African and everything to be proud of about that identity.

Many people are unaware that before the British had free and qualitative education in Great Britain, we were already implementing that policy in the Western region of Nigeria under that great sage, Chief Obafemi Awolowo.

Even more are yet unaware that before many in Europe and Asia came up with the idea of a single visa and economic free continental zone(EU/ASEAN), Kwame Nkrumah had already conceived of the idea and was advocating for one pan Africa without borders.

And Nimrod, that great empire builder who founded the world's very first empire in Babel was black being a descendant of Cush. He was the grandson of Ham (the progenitor of the Black race).

The reason contemporary Africans have not have lived up to this great ancestry is because we lack unity as a people.

Let me give a couple of examples. If the Prime Minister of Israel or any prominent Jewish leader from Israel is to visit the United States, they plan such a visit and consult with Jewish groups in the US such as the American Israel Public Affairs Committee (AIPAC). This ensures that Jews at home and in the Diaspora speak with one voice.

This and other groups were instrumental in arranging Benjamin Netanyahu's visit to the US Congress on the 3rd of March this year where the Israeli Prime Minister bypassed (some say snubbed) Obama and made Israel's case direct to Congress and the American people.

It took an immense amount of synergy between the State of Israel and the Jewish lobby in America to achieve this.

Arab leaders do the same thing with Arab lobby groups such as The American-Arab Anti-Discrimination Committee (ADC) and other bodies.

I am yet to see African leaders in politics and business do the same in an organized and consistent manner with the Black lobby and common interest groups in America such as the Congressional Black Caucus or The National Association for the Advancement of Colored People (NAACP) and other such groups.

We cannot get the respect and global voice we crave for as a people if we do not build a platform where black people the world over can speak with one voice.

We will remain shut out of permanent membership of the United Nations' Security Council if we don't blend our voice.

This is why I am very upset when African nations spar with each other, and recall ambassadors or fighting wars in the process.

The greatest affirmation of a racist's or a supremacist's thinking is actually the way and manner black people treat each other. Tribalism and Xenophobia, which are rampant in Africa, makes people with such inclinations think 'how can I like them if they don't like themselves'?

I support the outrage at recent and not so recent killings of black youths by White police officers and wannabe cops from the Trayvon Martin case to the incidences at Ferguson and Madison. But if truth be told, black on black violence is much higher in occurrence than these other incidences both in America and Africa.

The black world must address this by putting its house in order.

George Benson was right in his song 'The Greatest Love of All' when he said "learning to love yourself

It is the greatest love of all". No wonder the late Whitney Houston reprised it and made it an anthem. As Jesus said in John 8:32, 'you shall know the truth, and the truth shall make you free'.

Right now, I say to Nigeria, South Africa, the whole of Africa and the Black Race in the Diaspora, let us acquire that greatest love by exploring radical ideas.

Take Israel for example. On the 5th of July, 1950, Israel passed The Law of Return which gives people of Jewish ancestry, along with their spouses, the right to emigrate to Israel and obtain Israeli citizenship.

Perhaps nothing has built commitment to the cause of Israel worldwide than this single piece of legislation. Wealthy Jewish Americans, who have never been to Israel, die and leave their entire estates to the State of Israel to facilitate the implementation of this law.

Jews in sensitive positions in the West risk death and long prison sentences in order to spy for Israel in both military and industrial espionage.

Israel even granted Jonathan Pollard, an American Jew serving a life sentence for spying for Israel in the US, Israeli citizenship in 1995 while he was in jail.

Politicians of Jewish origin vote in Congress and the Parliaments of the West in ways that show their sympathy and even loyalty to Israel.

Why do they do this? Because Israel has, by The Law of Return, turned them from onlookers to stakeholders in the affairs of Israel.

This is what Africa must do. Instead of coming up with reasons why we do not like other black people because they are blacker or lighter or shorter or taller or nappier or straighter than us, the African Union must return to the Pan African ideas of the late Kwame Nkrumah, and act as a catalyst for a continental African Law of Return to be inserted into the Constitution of ALL African nations by ratification, giving people of African descent and their spouses the right to settle in any African nation of their choice and become full citizens.

If this is done, it will change the roles of the black African Diaspora in the West and everywhere from that of onlookers to a role as stakeholders in Africa. Eventually, the influx of returnees will become the first truly continental Africans with the ability to live and settle anywhere in Africa.

Once that happens, it will not be too long that xenophobia and tribalism will die a natural death.

I believe in this, and I, Ben Murray Bruce, will pursue and advance such ideas in the incoming 8th National Assembly because I believe the Legislature must be a place of ideas that will become laws that will change our nation and our continent for the better.

Published: 12th May, 2015.

CHAPTER 17
IT DOESN'T MATTER IF
THE CAT IS WHITE OR BLACK

Now that Major General Muhammadu Buhari (rtd) has been chosen by the Nigerian people, it is my duty as a patriotic Nigerian to help him succeed even though my candidate was President Goodluck Jonathan, a man to whom I will always be loyal and appreciative.

General Buhari is about to mount the saddle and I for one am in a very good position to tell him some home truths because as a senator-elect, I have a very fulfilling job awaiting me and I do not need a job or favours from Buhari so I do not have to play nice.

Looking at the personalities he has appointed to his transition council, I am wont to believe that General Buhari needs to expand his circle of friends and advisers.

As a military strategist, the president-elect must be familiar with the principle that the people you use in subduing an opponent are not necessarily the same persons you will need in rebuilding the territories you took. I may be using military terms, but I am sure General Buhari is aware that politics is war by other means and therefore many of the rules of war and peace apply to politics.

The General will be best served if he thinks of what is best for Nigeria rather than what is best for his party, the All Progressive Congress (APC), and its chieftains.

He must remember that in Nigeria's subjective politics, it was his person that the people voted for not his party and he should therefore serve the people the dish they are angling for.

And what are the expectations of Nigerians from General Buhari? Definitely not business as usual.

The president-elect ran on a promise of change and while that change was not really defined by its chanters, Nigerians defined it as a change in their situation.

To borrow from the famously potent prayers of Mountain of Fire and Miracle members, the Nigerian masses defined change as a situation where wealth and power must change hands from the elite to the masses by fire by force and they see General Buhari as the enforcer angel that will bring about this change.

With this type of expectation, Buhari's honeymoon period with Nigerians will not last very long if he does not take drastic steps to adjust Nigeria's economy to the realities of falling oil prices and a dearth of buyers for the Bonny Light Sweet Crude.

To put things into perspective, when the United States started buying less and less of Nigeria's oil, we looked to China as an alternative buyer of oil but it has since come to light that whereas America spent $101 billion on clean energy between 2012-13, China spent $125 billion within the same time frame.

The above data should alert Nigeria and other nations that look to China for oil markets to the fact that China is even ahead of the West in the search for alternative to fossil fuels as a source of energy.

Buhari may wish he did not win the 2015 elections when the reality of our economic situation sets in.

In his December 2014 Channels Television interview, Buhari said he was going to "stabilise the oil market". The General will learn soon enough that today's oil market is a buyers' market.

And the General's choices are limited because he cannot (unless he is extraordinarily brave and politically callous) do the obvious and sack civil servants. Yes, he will eventually have to reduce the over bloated federal civil service, but before he can do that, he has to build up political capital by reducing the overhead of the Executive and persuade the Legislature to follow suit.

Austerity measures must start from Aso Rock. This means that luxurious multi car convoys must be reduced. The presidential air fleet has to go, by way of being auctioned off or sold to local airlines. Estacode allowances must be slashed and the president's entourages should be lean while non-essential foreign travels should be banned.

The president-elect should not underestimate the big difference these small changes can make and their capacity to buy him enough credibility with the labour unions, the kind of credibility that will see them accepting cuts in the federal workforce and reduction in pay and entitlements.

A small change like flying commercial instead of by private jet saved Britain a whopping £200,000 when the thrifty British Prime Minister, David Cameron, flew to America to meet President Barack Obama on a regular BA flight.

Nigeria is in for very desperate times if we do not tighten our belts while our major foreign exchange earner is facing global challenges.

Russia, a nation that many will say is more prepared than Nigeria for the shocks occasioned by the drop in the price of oil devalued its currency by 11 per cent in just one day.

While Russia is taking these steps, the world is watching to see if Nigeria will continue to spend hundreds of billions annually sponsoring its elite on pilgrimages to Mecca and Jerusalem.

I mean, no economist will get why a nation with over 60 percent of its people living in poverty at the best of times, will spend almost 1 per cent of its annual budget sponsoring pilgrimages for its elite who can afford to go to the Holy Land on their own dime.

I for one do not get it. A pilgrimage is meant to be a sacrifice of a believer. How is a pilgrimage still a sacrifice when someone pays for you to go? The Nigerian government is sending people on holidays not pilgrimages!

I daresay that the money being spent by the Nigerian government to airlift pilgrims to both Holy Lands is enough to educate all the almajiri in Northern Nigeria. Wouldn't God and humanity be better served if we looked after the less privileged in our midst?

General Buhari has his work cut out for him and he does not have time to be bitter about who said what, when and where. He must let go of any desire to pay any of his traducers back whether they be from the last 16 years or as far back as 1985.

Four years is only enough time to fix Nigeria. Any time spent on other ventures is time taken from this most important of assignments.

And let me say that General Buhari should not allow himself to be pigeon holed by people who dangle ideologies instead of realities. Yes, the APC may have styled itself as a progressive party, which in itself is a contradiction because Buhari is a conservative, but Buhari should not bother about that.

Whether the philosophy is progressive or conservative or liberal or free market, he should go with what works because as Deng Xiaoping once noted: "It doesn't matter whether a cat is black or white, if it catches mice it is a good cat."

And it is fitting for me to end with a mention of Xiaoping. No other contemporary world leader, in my opinion, closely mirrors Buhari as does Xiaoping.

In 1966, Xiaoping was dethroned from his powerful party positions by loyalists of Chairman Mao as was Buhari in 1985 by loyalists of his Chief of Army staff.

Xiaoping suffered house arrest, loss of earned privileges and was consigned to political limbo for almost a decade as was Buhari.

But then Xiaoping bounced back into favour and became China's leader in 1976 and thereafter jettisoned his life long belief in Mao's Cultural Revolution and introduced the "one country, two systems" policy that allowed communism and capitalism to coexist in China. This is similar to Buhari's conversion from an anti-democrat who believed power flowed from the barrel of a gun to a democrat who accepted democracy as the best form of governance and capitalism as the natural economic policy of a democracy.

But this is where Buhari has to learn from Xiaoping. Xiaoping refused to demonise Chairman Mao, his predecessor who had purged him from power and placed him under house arrest after stripping him off his privileges. Instead of bitterness, Xiaoping believed that Mao's "accomplishments must be considered before his mistakes".

This is how Buhari must treat his predecessors. He must not demonise everything that was done by previous administrations and mark those who served in those government as persona non grata. He must take the bitter with the sweet and make use of the best brains Nigeria has to offer, for as he said on December 31st, 1983, "This generation of Nigerians and indeed future generations have no other country than Nigeria".

Published: 29th April, 2015.

Chapter 18
The Nigeria of Our Dreams:
Never Forgotten Angels

Being a speech delivered by the distinguished Senator Ben Murray Bruce at the occasion of the 10th Anniversary Celebration of the 60 Angels of Loyola Jesuit College on November 29th, 2015.

I thank you for inviting me to this tenth anniversary celebration of your and our sixty angels who passed away on the 10th of December 2005 in Port Harcourt, Rivers State.

In honour of their memory, I would like to ask all of us to please stand and observe a minute's silence.

Children are very important in the cycle of life. In one of my favourite songs, 'The Greatest Love of All' sung by both George Benson and Whitney Houston, the song writer said:

"I believe the children are our future.

Teach them well and let them lead the way. Show them all the beauty they possess inside. Give them a sense of pride to make it easier. Let the children's laughter remind us how we used to be."

This is a message we need to hear in Nigeria again and again because we, and by we I mean the elite, of which I am one, have monumentally failed this nation.

I remember when I was the Director General of the Nigerian Television Authority, NTA, I read an interview in ThisDay Newspapers about the son of a particular former Nigerian leader who talked about how much he loves his polo horse to the extent that when it was sick he flew the horse to Switzerland for treatment at an outrageous price.

Now, I happen to have visited some of the communities around the mansion where this child of privilege lives and it is peopled with children who go to some of the most horrendous schools you can imagine.

Some of these schools do not have enough desks. Some do not even have complete roofs. All of them do not have enough teachers.

Yet we have the son of a man who once ruled this nation spending lavishly on a horse while schools within his radius are crumbling.

Now the reason I mention this is because his father once gave an interview in the same ThisDay Newspapers in which he revealed that he achieved the height he reached in life because of the free and qualitative education he received from Nigeria in the 50s and 60s!

Why do our elite behave this way? Why do we climb the ladder of success that was freely given to us and then remove it when we get to the top?

Why do we enjoy the shade that good men from yesterday planted for us only to uproot the trees instead of planting more?

You see, I think we do this because as a nation we have lost our ability to empathize with the poorest Nigerians for the simple reason that our elite are not stake holders in Nigeria.

When you move about with armed policemen who block you from the common man and block the common man from you, how can you empathize with him?

When your children school abroad and you never bother to know where the children of your driver and your cook go to school, how can you empathize with them?

When you are flown to Europe for a headache and you never patronize the general hospital in your state, how can you empathize with the masses?

Today, we are fighting terrorism in Nigeria and we are focusing on a military battle with guns and bullets.

But the truth is that over the years, Nigeria has neglected the children of the peasants in the Northeast of Nigeria to the extent that 52.4% of males in the Northeastern region of Nigeria have no formal Western education whatsoever.

If a nation will not spend her wealth educating her youth, that nation will spend the same wealth fighting insecurity amongst those same youth.

If we had spent the billions we are now spending to fight terrorism in educating ALL Nigerian children in the 80s, we would not be spending trillions fighting terrorists today.

Lets plan for tomorrow!

What we need are policies that will force our elite to become stakeholders in Nigeria and only then would they be able to empathize with what the average Nigerian goes through.

I propose that the President should start this empathy revolution by ordering that his minister of education must educate his children in Nigeria and that his minister of health must patronize our local health facilities.

This will have the effect of turning them to stakeholders. Currently they are only onlookers. Stakeholders empathize. Onlookers are indifferent.

I believe that the 8th National Assembly, of which I am a part, must pass a bill to make it mandatory that education must have the highest sectoral allocation in every budget cycle at the federal level.

You see, the cycle of poverty in Nigeria is going to continue if we do not build more schools like the Loyola Jesuit College all over Nigeria.

And I must commend the Jesuits. Ever since Saint Ignatius Loyola founded this esteemed order, they continue to make this world a better place by moulding the minds of youths all over the world through moral and intellectual education.

I call on the Federal and State Governments to come to the Jesuits to learn how not to waste the minds of our youths.

When they learn that lesson, terrorism will become a thing of the past and the young man who takes his horse to Switzerland for treatment can ride it openly without the fear of been blown to smithereens by terrorists.

Recently, some Nigerians took to putting French flags on their Social Media profiles to identify with and remember those who died during the recent Paris attacks.

It is sad that while we want to identify and remember those who are very far away from us, we do not seem moved enough to put Nigerian flags on our profiles when terrorists strike in Nigeria or when tragedy befalls us.

I am glad to say that the teachers and parents of the Loyola Jesuit College are an exception to this behaviour and you are a beacon of hope and a silver lining on often cloudy days.

Once again I commend you for what you have done for education in Nigeria and even more so for how you have kept alive the memory of the 60 angels who lost their lives on that tragic day in 2005.

In their honour, permit me to read this poem by Kechi Okwuchi, your former student and one of only two survivors of that tragedy:

A Tribute to the Angels

By KECHI OKWUCHI

It seems like yesterday
Full of excitement
We chatted non-stop
All the way to the plane
It seems like yesterday
We made plans, discarded them
Made new ones
Our future bright
It seems like yesterday
When we dropped out of the sky
To noise, to pain, to...silence
To glory
It seems like yesterday
That God had different plans
To take us to greater heights
A future not foreseen
On angels' wings we flew
Racing past the clouds
Racing up to glory
Enveloped by His Grace
Though not with you in glory
I am a part of you
Left behind to continue the legacy
Left to run the race
As long as there is breathe in me
Dearest 60, you are not forgotten
Through the pain of yesterday
A million tomorrows are born.

Thank you for inviting me to this most honourable of events. May God bless you and may God bless Nigeria.

Chapter 19
Five Thousand Naira is Possible

One of the best policies I have ever come across in Nigeria's electioneering history, is the promised policy of the All Progressive Congress to pay the sum of ₦5,000 monthly as Job Seekers Allowance for unemployed Nigerian youths.

It is a policy with the proverbial human face and whoever suggested it to the All Progressive Party probably won the election for them and must be commended.

The fact that Nigeria has no social security system is one of the reasons why there is so much desperation in our nation with the consequence that crime and ethnic and religious crises are a sad reality of life in many parts of the nation.

I give my whole hearted support to this policy and I promise that I will do all I can possibly do to make it a reality.

However, this promised policy is under threat because some of us do not believe it is practicable. Nothing could be further from the truth.

It is possible to fulfill this promise and I will articulate how Nigeria can do it.

The biggest argument against the policy is that Nigeria does not have the database required to make it work.

This argument, if it is not mischievous, is based on inadequate knowledge of the resources available to the government. In fact, the opposite is very much true. As at 2015, Nigeria has more than enough Information based technology to make this policy a reality.

In today's Nigeria, particularly after the cashless policy introduced under the former Central Bank of Nigeria governor and now emir of Kano, HRM Muhammadu Sanusi, every graduate has a bank account with a Bank Verification Number.

In addition to that, they each should have a Permanent Voter Card. Additionally they may also have a National ID Card.

Each of these platforms are connected to a database which can identify each graduate by their bio data and trace their whereabouts through their phones.

By law, every Nigerian graduate under the age of 30 must serve his country under the National Youth Service Corp, NYSC, scheme and the NYSC gives them a call up letter with which they register these youths and capture their bio-data.

So whichever way you want to look at it, there are databases that can identify fresh graduates in Nigeria at any given time. It is almost impossible that a graduate will not be captured in at least one of either the BVN, PVC, National ID or NYSC database.

The next question is how will the government know which of these graduates are employed and which are not?

It is possible.

First the government must include in the law setting up the job seekers allowance the proviso that if you are caught fraudulently collecting the assistance you will get a mandatory jail sentence.

Thereafter, the government should introduce criteria for applying for the allowance which should, in my opinion, only be open to graduates who have passed out of the NYSC Programme and should be accessible for no longer than two years after passing out from the Programme.

Now, within those two years, the Federal Government can verify whether or not graduates who are registered under the job seekers allowance have regular income from the activity of their bank accounts. The Central Bank has access to their account activity. If they have regular monthly payments, then they are obviously employed and government will not pay them.

But then you may ask, where would the money come from?

Like other nations, those that have must support those that do not have.

Every employed Nigerian should pay an unemployment tax of between 2% (for lower income earners) to 5% (for middle to high income earners) to help pay ₦5,000 to unemployed graduates.

This is a sacrifice we must make which will have a positive effect on our economy and will also drastically reduce crime.

Nigeria was able to help over 11 million farmers access inexpensive fertilizer under the e-wallet fertilizer distribution scheme of the ministry of Agriculture when Dr. Akinwumi Adesina was minister.

If we could do this then, we can certainly handle the logistics of paying job seekers allowance to our unemployed graduates.

If the will is there on the part of the President Muhammadu Buhari led administration, this idea can revolutionize Nigeria and help reduce extreme poverty in Nigeria. It should be supported by all Nigerians irrespective of party, tribe or religion.

My support for this Programme has nothing to do with politics. I believe in empowering youths. Recently Silverbird opened a new cinema in Festac town which will give direct employment to 50 Nigerian youths and indirect employment to hundreds more.

However, this is just a drop in the ocean. There are millions of youths, many of whom are graduates and try as we may, we will not be able to immediately provide jobs for all of them.

What happens to those of them without jobs? What if their parents also do not have jobs? How will they feed? Obviously ₦5,000 cannot feed a graduate for a month. But at least it is better than nothing.

Finally, I commend the wife of the President, Mrs. Aisha Buhari, for her support for this promised policy to be kept. Mrs. Buhari, by that gesture, has validated the proverb which says behind every great man, there is an equally great woman.

My name is Ben Murray Bruce and I just want to make common sense!

Chapter 20
Freedom of Information as Freedom to be Powerful

Being a speech delivered by the distinguished Senator Ben Murray Bruce at the occasion of the e-Nigeria 2015 summit held by the National Information Technology Development Agency on November 17th, 2001.

Protocols.

Something historical and earth shattering happened in Nigeria on the 31st of May, 2011. On that day, Nigeria's then President, Dr. Goodluck Jonathan, signed the Freedom of Information Act into law.

The expectation of media practitioners like myself and many others is that that law would lift the veil on governance and demystify the kitchen cabinets, bureaucracies and red tape that make all the behind the scene moves in the corridors of power.

From my personal conversations with Western Diplomats and investors, I can also say with confidence that they also had similar expectations.

However, those expectations have not materialized and for all the activism and pressure that the civil rights community brought to bear on government to pass that bill into law, there has been a failure on their part and on the part of the larger Nigerian community to live up to the expectation of that law.

The Freedom of Information law was meant to democratize access to information and promote transparency in governance and in the private sector. The whole idea was that since corruption breeds in secrecy, then transparency would be like starving corruption off oxygen.

When our brother, Kofi Annan, said "knowledge is power. Information is liberating", he was re echoing something that philosophers have been telling us since the time of Francis Bacon, and that is that 'Information is Power'.

The reason many Nigerian citizens feel powerless is because our activists and advocates have not made the best use of the FOI Law up until now.

Let me say for the avoidance of doubt that Nigerians have a right to information on how they are governed.

But despite the fact that we have this right, too many things are still shrouded in secrecy.

Over the past two years for instance, controversy was stirred because of allegations and denials on whether or not $49.8 billion or $20 billion or $12 billion was missing.

Questions like how much Nigeria really spends on fuel subsidy and how much income the nation makes and what percentage of it should be paid into the federation account should not have even arisen after 2011.

More importantly, in 2015 we are still dealing with the issue of access to election materials and information on both the part of the petitioner and the respondents in our Election Petition Tribunals.

The whole basis of the Freedom of Information Law is that there should be a free flow of information and I for one find it most troubling that when the results of an election are in dispute before a court, the issue of access to any kind of information regarding that election could still be in dispute. That should be a given.

Information cannot be manipulated for whatever reason, when it is totally available. You can only manipulate information that is selectively available.

The job of the National Information Technology Development Agency (NITDA) in my opinion, should be to develop technology that would help promote access to information about government, the private sector, the media and the society in general.

The purpose of such technology would be to advance the progress and development of Nigeria by empowering Nigerians, our government and our development partners with information that both simplifies and reduces the cost of our interactions, first, with each other in Nigeria, and then with the world.

You wanted me to speak on the theme of a Comparative Analysis of Nigeria's 2015 Election With Existing Global Best High Tech Electronic Electoral Process in a Developed Economy.

Many people erroneously assume that the reason the West seemingly has better elections than we do is because they have better access to technology.

That would not be a correct assumption.

The reason the West has better elections than we do in Africa is because they have freedom of information which leads to transparency and transparency builds trust and where there is trust, the price of everything, including elections, business and governance, reduces while their value increases.

Therefore, to have better elections which will automatically increase trust in Nigeria, I am convinced that what we need to do is to empower our citizens economically because when citizens are economically empowered there is a significant reduction in their susceptibility to participate in electoral fraud and malpractices.

In fact, studies show that the wealthier a nation is the more credible its electoral process.

The 2015 elections have come and gone and whatever you and I might think about the results, the verdict of Independent Electoral Observers is that those elections were the freest and most credible elections since Nigeria returned to civil rule and possibly the best we have ever had since 1957.

Could it be a coincidence that the 2015 elections were held at the time Nigeria became the largest economy in Africa and at a time when Per Capita Income was the highest it has ever been since 1999?

Remember, studies show that the wealthier a nation is the more credible its electoral process.

Could it be a coincidence that the 2015 Presidential election remains the only election of which the candidate who lost did not challenge the victory of the winning candidate in court?

I do not think so.

So rather than focus on the theme of a Comparative Analysis of Nigeria's 2015 Election, I would rather prepare for a better election in 2019 by discussing how Information Technology, which was one of the keys (but not the only one) to the increased credibility of the 2015 elections, can be used to improve the fortunes of the average Nigerian so that by 2019, our people would be wealthier and as a result we would have a more credible poll.

For instance, Nigeria has millions of her citizens and people of Nigerian heritage living all over the world.

Of the $50 billion that was repatriated to Africa by Africans last year, slightly under 50% of that amount was repatriated by Nigerians who send money back home to friends and family or to set up one business or the other.

Many Africans and Nigerians, including our government, celebrate that as a major feat, but while this patriotic action must be commended, what has gone unnoticed is the fact that whereas Western Union, the chief money transfer vehicle for Africa and world, charges citizens of G-20 nations a 5% commission to transfer funds and 7.8% for citizens of other nations, the same Western Union charges Nigerians and others wishing to transfer money to sub-Saharan African nations 12%!

In fact, that is the good news. Other lesser known money transfer vehicles even charge a higher premium for the same service.

When I queried the reason for this discrepancy in charges, it was revealed that the cost of wiring money to Nigeria and sub-Saharan Africa is higher because of a higher risk for fraud due to lapses and gaps in our ability to digitally identify and trace our citizens.

Now, this is where the National Information Technology Development Agency can come in.

Our problem, as I said earlier, is not lack of information, but rather it is imprisonment of information instead of freedom of information.

As we all know, due to the commendable work of the former Independent National Electoral Commission, INEC, Chairman, Professor Attahiru Jega, and his team, there are now 80 million Permanent Voter Cards in the hands of adult Nigerians. This represents 50% of our estimated population.

In addition, all account holding Nigerians now either have or are in the process of having a Bank Verification Number, BVN.

Even further, millions of Nigerians have collected their National Identity Card.

The PVC, the National ID Card and the BVN have the complete identity details and traceable bio data of all Nigerians who use them.

I have it on good authority that if NITDA, as the premier Information Technology Czar of Nigeria, would galvanize the rest of Nigeria's Information Technology dependent bodies like the Nigerian Communications Commission, NCC, the Nigerian Identity Management Commission,

NIMC, as well as the Central Bank of Nigeria, CBN, to make a corporate petition to Western Union's Head Office to the effect that Nigeria has the infrastructure to digitally identify and trace the identity and whereabouts of her adult population, Western Union, upon confirmation of the existence and accuracy of these infrastructure, would then be duty bound to reduce commissions for money transfers to Nigeria from 12% to at least 7.8% and possibly 5%.

What this means is that repatriation to Nigeria would automatically increase by between 5-7% which translates to a capital inflow of between $800 million to $1 billion annually.

Hello NITDA, did you catch that!

Pause for effect.

Do you now see what Sir Francis Bacon meant when he said 'information is power'?

In the United States, the Durst Organization maintains a National Debt Clock, which monitors the national debt of the US, thus increasing awareness for the government, the opposition and the citizenry, so that no one can manipulate information on how much America makes and what she owes and to whom.

NITDA does not have to reinvent the wheel. What are you set up for? To develop information technology.

If NITDA can set up right here in Abuja, a clock that informs Nigerians in real time, how much Nigeria has made from oil and from other means and how much we owe and the extent of our budget implementation and the amount of surplus or deficit it runs, NITDA would in one fell swoop have promoted so much transparency and openness which will definitely dramatically improve Nigeria's rating in Transparency International's Corruption Perception Index, which would in turn mean a reduction in the cost of doing business in Nigeria.

Hello NITDA, did you catch that!

Pause for effect.

Do you now see what Kofi Annan meant when he said 'information is liberating'?

In the 50s, 60s, 70s and 80s, tyrants use to be dictators who governed with iron fists and by authoritarian fiats.

Not any more. Today, modern day tyranny comes from the secreting or hoarding of knowledge or information which Robin Morgan described as "tyranny camouflaged as humility".

Indeed, the world Super Powers and global blocs have been trying for decades to topple dictators that had sometime been in power for decades.

They had sent in armies and failed. They sent in propaganda and failed. They poured in money to dissidents and rebels and failed spectacularly.

Then some young boys in the Silicon Valley region of California globally democratized access to information through Google, YouTube, Facebook, Twitter and a host of others and these daughters of Information Technology did what armies, what propaganda, what money and what Rebels could not do.

They brought freedom to a people under tyranny.

You see, information exposes the truth and as is now commonly known, "you shall know the truth and the truth will make you free".

In Nigeria's case, we already have a law that gives us freedom. But you may say it is just freedom of information. But do not forget that information is power.

If the law gives you freedom of information, it also gives you freedom to be powerful.

One of the founders of Pan Africanism, Kwame Nkrumah, was famous for saying "Seek ye first the political kingdom, and all else shall be added unto you".

Today, we have seen how mistaken we were because many African nations are politically independent yet remain economically dependent.

Upon deeper reflection, it seems truer today to say "Seek ye first the economic kingdom, and all else shall be added unto you".

All else includes a more transparent and credible election and it all begins with ensuring that information is freely available avid freely shared within Nigeria.

Thank you very much for inviting me and may God bless the National Information Technology Development Agency and may God bless Nigeria.

CHAPTER 21
OF BUHARI AND COMMAND PRESENCE

When President Harry S. Truman put the sign 'The Buck Stops Here' on his desk at the Oval Office of the White House, he was reminding himself and all future Presidents that by virtue of the office they occupy, they lose the right to complain and gripe because they are at the top of the politics food chain and at that level they talk in terms of solution not in the reactive language of blamers.

When a President or a Governor complains or blames others for problems they are facing, they are actually communicating helplessness.

When you complain, you are indicating that you are powerless to change the situation. When you blame others you are declaring that their weaknesses have overwhelmed your capacity.

It is not seemly for leaders to gripe or complain. What leaders should do is change the situation or change their attitude to it.

You can only blame your predecessor for your problems for so long. After 6 months, so long becomes too long! 6 months is 1/8 of a 4 year tenure. If you are still blaming your predecessor after 6 months, when are you going to deliver the goods?

When you complain within your country, you undermine your authority. As a leader, it is even worse when you go overseas to complain. Rather than sympathy, what happens is that you undermine your country's sovereignty.

Imagine that a man is married and has a wife and children and he observes some defects in the way his house is being ran. Suppose that rather than address the identified problems he instead complains about it to his wife. Invariably what he is telling his wife is that he is incapable of wearing the trousers in the house.

But then suppose that he goes to his neighbor's house to complain. Yes, the neighbor, if he is polite, would listen politely and make all the right noises.

But as soon as the man returns home, the neighbor will from that moment know that that man is not man enough to face up to his problems and his respect for him will evaporate.

Nigeria is an independent nation. We have been so for the last 55 years. We are not under any colonial master. Thus, we should not make our problem the problem of other nations.

Every nation has problems, however, it is the job of the leader of that nation to tell the outside world the good things about his nation. A President is the chief ambassador of his country. He is the face of the nation.

Major General Mamman Jiya Vatsa was my very good friend. I was with him two days before he was arrested by the Babangida administration.

I will never forget what he said during his trial for treason. He warned the Nigeria that the moment you start to insult yourself, you will never be in short supply of people willing to join you.

We must stop insulting ourselves to the outside world.

Our value as a people is tied to the value of Nigeria. If we think we are devaluing our predecessors by telling anyone who cares to listen that their shortcomings is the reason for our lack of progress we will be wrong and terribly so.

What we will be doing is diminishing the status of Nigeria to the rest of the world and that loss of status affects us all.

Those blaming Jonathan and the Peoples Democratic Party for theirs and the nation's woes should realize that a prophet is always honored abroad.

Jonathan just returned from Tanzania where the Commonwealth of Nations entrusted him to lead their election observer mission that monitored presidential election in the East African nation.

They searched the length and breadth of Africa and the man they found with the moral authority to overshadow the democratic process in Tanzania was Jonathan.

While in Tanzania, the two largest papers in that country showered praises on him in their editorials.

The Daily News of Tanzania wrote that "Jonathan may very well have averted bloodshed that is characteristic of incumbent leaders who cling in power tooth and nail, fang and claw! What lesson is there in this for us in Tanzania, pray?"

The Guardian of Tanzania in an editorial noted that "Jonathan's voluntary handover of power to the opposition wrote a new chapter for Nigeria's democracy, given the fact that it is rare for sitting presidents in Africa to hand over powers to winning opposition parties."

So, no matter what anybody may say to the world about President Goodluck Jonathan and the PDP, the world also has its own way of getting independent information on Nigeria.

Hate him or love him, Jonathan has left giant footprints in eternity's sands of time!

And it is not only foreigners that are hailing Jonathan. On the day he returned to Nigeria, his new media spokesman, Reno Omokri, tweeted a picture of him arriving and said "Welcome home ex-President GEJ. You did us proud in Tanzania. May your days be long and useful in serving the world." "This is the #faceofdemocracy in Africa, ex President Goodluck Jonathan of Nigeria who loved not power at all cost!".

That tweet went viral and was retweeted hundreds of times by Nigerians and foreigners alike and sparked a Vanguard Newspaper headline, 'Nigerians Hail Jonathan Over Tanzania Polls".

Jonathan and the PDP have done their bit and nobody can write them out of history. It is actually better for the incumbent to move on and achieve greater things and stop making Jonathan the issue in Nigerian and global politics.

Let us take President Barrack Obama as an example. He was elected President of the United States at the age of 47. At the time of his inauguration, the world was grappling with a global recession due in large part to the policies of his predecessor in office. Yet, President Obama never blamed his predecessor for the woes of America.

Rather, he acknowledged the good that President George W Bush did and knowing that the buck stopped at his desk, he went on to introduce policies that jump started the US and the world economy and today, under his guidance, the US and the world has come out from an unprecedented global depression that almost crippled Wall Street, to a period of economic prosperity which has seen global poverty reduce to its lowest ever level of below 10%.

That is the stuff of which leadership is made of. A leader takes responsibility. He should not take the easy way out.

I am a keen student of the concept of leadership and the very bottom line of leadership is influence.

To gain influence, a leader must know where he wants to take his country and must have the influence to persuade the citizens of his nation to cooperate with him in making the journey to his desired destination.

To get their buy in, a leader must inspire his citizens to have confidence in him, their nation and in themselves.

The words of a leader carry weight. A wrong word can affect the value of the Stock Exchange and the overall GDP.

I recommend the practice of Command Presence to Nigerian leaders. A command presence is a leadership posture which while it does not communicate that it has all the solution it still project confidence that a solution will be found.

It encompasses the practice of speaking and acting with confidence and power. It is avoiding sounding apologetic or inadequate to the challenges at hand.

Let me give a graphic example of a Command Presence.

On the morning of September 11, 2001, President George W Bush was reading to a class at the Emma E Booker elementary school in Sarasota, Florida, when then White House Chief of Staff, Andrew Card, approached him and whispered into his ears the news that America had been attacked by terrorists and that the second tower of the World Trade Center had been hit.

President Bush did not miss a beat. He remained calm as though he had not been told anything alarming. The news cameras were trained on him and for seven minutes he continued to read to the children. After reading to them, he calmly got up and left the building to address a press conference to reassure Americans of their safety and that the US would bring the culprits to book.

While it was Bush who gave that assurance, it was Obama who got Osama Bin Laden, proving that governance is a continuum not a competition.

Had Bush shown panic upon hearing the news, that panic would have permeated America and weakened their military and economy as well as any other institutions America relies on for strength. But because he projected strength and calmness, the nation he led rallied behind him and put their attackers to shame!

That is a Command Presence worthy of an Oscar award. Nigerian leaders should take a cue from President Bush's behavior.

To paraphrase the Singer, Omawumi, if a leader complains to me, na who I go complain to?

During the Second World War, almost all of Britain's elite fighting force and armory was about to be lost to Germany at Dunkirk in France between May and June 1940.

Privately, the then British leader, Winston Churchill, told Parliament the incidence was "a colossal military disaster" and that "the whole root and core and brain of the British Army" was either to perish or be captured by the Germans.

But even at this most cataclysmic time in British history, Churchill maintained a Command Presence. He did not lie to the British public. No.

He gave a broadcast to the British nation and her allies and buoyed them up with a 'yes we can' message. And what was the result? Britain, like the Phoenix, rose from the ashes of defeat to, with the aid of her allies, crush her enemy.

Allies, whether they be economic or military, will only support a leader that believes in himself and his country. Complaining leaders make them nervous which may explain the disturbing level of capital flight out of Nigeria.

President Buhari must accept that Nigeria is facing an economic trial of epic proportions and that he was elected President at such a time as this because Nigerians knew that President Buhari possessed the capacity to lead the nation out of the present storm.

It is now up to President Buhari to put the confidence the Nigerian people reposed in him to good use and consider projecting a Command Presence that projects confidence at home and abroad.

The President must be wary of those people that tell him that all the challenges he is grappling with are ex-President Jonathan's fault.

Boko Haram has killed at least 1700 people since his inauguration, International ratings agencies have downgraded us because according to them Nigeria lacks a clear "economic direction" and an elder statesman and head of one of the ethnic nationalities that make up Nigeria was kidnapped, cut with a machete and beaten to a pulp.

These are not the doings of Jonathan or the PDP.

Finally, those of us who advise President Muhammadu Buhari to make hay while the sun shines are his friends. It is unwise to make blame while the sun shines.

Above all, the President must remember that wounds from a sincere friend are better than many kisses from an enemy.

My name is Ben Murray Bruce and I just want to make common sense!

Ben Bruce is the Senator representing Bayelsa East in the National Assembly as well as Chairman of the Silverbird Entertainment Group.

www.ingramcontent.com/pod-product-compliance
Lightning Source LLC
Chambersburg PA
CBHW070116300326
41934CB00035B/1351